I Tell You the Truth

"Come and see," said Jesus.

"I Am The Truth."

Larry Kennedy

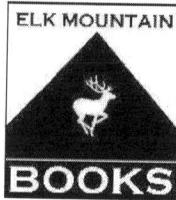

Published by:

ELK MOUNTAIN

BOOKS

Elk Mountain Books

info@elkmountianbooks.com

ISBN Print Edition: 1497448948

EAN-13: 978-1497448940

ACKNOWLEDGEMENTS

I would like to acknowledge several people who have helped me along in this process. First my "cousin in law" in Alaska who was the first editor and so encouraged me; and to Dwight Royer who did more editing; to Perry Perkins who has been both publisher and encourager, with whom I hope to continue with a second book on *The Beauty of the Lord*; and finally to my wife, Laurie, whose hard work as a nurse case manager has allowed me the time and space to pursue my writing. Without her, years of fruitful ministry would not have been possible.

Last but not least to my Lord who has been ever faithful through the valleys and the mountains of my life.

May this discussion of Jesus as, The Truth, draw you ever and ever closer to Him and ever proclaiming Him as truth to people in your circle of influence who so desperately need Him.

In His service,

Larry

Introduction

Perhaps like me, you are weary of hearing the spin doctors giving their slant on the truth. CNN give their version and Fox give theirs.

The representatives are often so mean-spirited, especially on the conservative side, that the atmosphere is saturated with venom.

The media mantra seems to be; if there is no controversy, make one up. I notice that now the Oregonian (*and I am sure other newspapers*) have a section dedicated to evaluating the truth spoken by candidates for office or other public officials.

Usually the evaluation's end result is that what the official said is partly true and partly false.

Perhaps like me you want to shout from the rooftop, "won't someone simply tell the truth?"

Falsehood and hedging has many faces.

If falsehood, like truth, had but one face, we would be on more equal terms, for we would consider the contrary of what the liar said to be certain. But the opposite of truth has a hundred thousand faces and an infinite field. [1]

We deal with shades of truth and falsehood continually. There was a time when we expected people in authority to be truthful.

But that time is long past. We have seen too many shades the truth, and lie with impunity.

We have as a result, several cynical generations who now believe everyone is "on the take," and everyone is affected with some hidden besetting sin which often leads to the abuse of others.

This cynicism shows no favoritism. It spans across the board to anyone in positions of authority, even to one's neighbor.

This cynicism and skepticism overflows into the realm of ultimate truth also.

There is much confusion in regard to their being a God of truth. According to Gallop polls there are some 90% of the people in America who believe in God. The polls also reveal that it only makes a difference in about 15% of those "believers" regarding how they live and make decisions.

This statistic begs the question, if He is God, then should not what He says be considered absolute truth?

Ought not His boundaries, directions and plans for us, be followed as such?

The problem is that current philosophical ethics has long ago ruled out absolute truth and shifted totally to a contextual ethic. What is wrong in one circumstance may be right under changing circumstances.

Except for Christian teachers, those who hold that persuasion are the ones teaching our children from kindergarten through college.

Not only is God no longer addressed in prayer, though certainly children can pray on their own and ought to be encouraged to do so, but the absence of any discussion of God or His perspective of right and wrong are considered off limits for public education.

The message to the students is that He does not matter enough to discuss even as a possibility, although it is acceptable to discuss other theories. To discuss *Him* in school is seen to be illegal.

Not only that, but to espouse any view that there is such a thing as absolute truth is considered archaic, ignorant or at the very least superstitious blind obedience to a world view long ago abandoned. Those who hold such views are lumped together as Bible thumping fundamentalists.

Sadly, our insensitivity has given the public plenty of ammunition for those overgeneralizations.

Often those of the religious right have vilified those whom they oppose as the enemy.

Even though we may not agree with other viewpoints, people are not enemies. They are the ones for whom Jesus came and lived and died. We have forgotten that mercy triumphs over judgment.

The truth is, that truth when heard, changes everything. The truth is that if there is a God as revealed in the Holy Bible, we will have to change our lives and perspectives about what we are doing here in this space-time-existence.

Maybe we "can't handle the truth," like the officer said in "A Few Good Men."

Churchill said, *"Men occasionally stumble over the truth, but most of them pick themselves up and hurry off as if nothing had happened."*

Even in Jesus' time and ministry there were those who rejected the truth. The Apostle Paul described them in the first chapter of Romans. They are those who "hold the truth in unrighteousness." That is, they know the truth but deny it because it is too uncomfortable for them. It is "the unbearable light of being" that exposes our very hearts.

Jesus said he knew the hearts of men, that they loved darkness more than light. The Lord says, "I speak only what is true and right,"[2].

"What is truth?" Pilate asked Jesus. How ironic! The very essence and embodiment of truth is asked sarcastically if truth exists!

Truth is standing before you, Pilate. He is a Person. In Jesus the "Spirit of Truth" dwells.

He describes Himself as "the Way, the Truth and Life." Just before His so-called trial, He promised to send His disciples the "Spirit of Truth," the "Counselor," and "Comforter," who would come after Jesus had ascended to glory.

They were to wait in Jerusalem for "power from on High." They had no idea what that meant. They would know it when it happened.

They must simply be obedient to do what Jesus had said: pray and wait. The Spirit of Truth would guide them and remind them of all Jesus had said and done.

Even the antagonistic listeners testified that, "This man speaks with authority."

Soldiers sent to arrest him came back empty-handed saying, "No one ever spoke like this man." Something in His demeanor on the cross at Calvary caused the soldier to exclaim, "Surely this was the Son of God." When He spoke, the Word of God was flowing forth; resonating in people's hearts like a wooden instrument resonates at the plucking or striking of strings. There is a bearing witness that this Person is the Voice of Truth by which we were created. Truth seekers respond like a newborn child responds to His mother's voice having heard it already in the womb.

He is the Eternal Word whose desire is to reveal Himself, not mask himself. Oscar Wilde said, "Man is least himself when he talks in his own person. Give him a mask, and he will tell you the truth."

But Jesus was radiantly transparent to those who were authentically seeking truth.

When His voice speaks forth, He cannot but speak truth. Anything less than truth would mean He is not God the Son.

Truth is that which explains and lines up with reality, the way things are in this time space existence and, how they relate to the unseen.

Quantum physics now says there are other realms, perhaps as many as eleven dimensions, not just the classic four dimensions with which we are so comfortable. The Apostle Paul said, first the physical, then the spiritual. Spiritually, there are unseen realms that are related to the visible realms. These unseen realms interact with our time space continuum, a parallel existence if you will.

Paul speaks frankly about this unseen world in His letters to Ephesus, Colossi and Corinth. He says God's purpose was "to show his wisdom in all its rich variety to all the rulers and authorities in the heavenly realms", through His united Church (Jew and Non-Jew) joined together as His fellowship, His family[3].

This was His plan from the beginning, now carried out through Christ Jesus our Lord.

He taught that His kingdom is within us by reason of His indwelling Spirit. It is not something we can conjure up. It is not earth-born. It is God-born. It is a gift through Christ.

"This kingdom," said the Lord "is not of this world." Yet within this world, He has given his followers authority. By faith, they are to tear down evil mindsets and affect earth's direction toward kingdom purposes.

His followers are invisible nations within nations. Kingdom-authorized believers empowered with the ministry of reconciliation to do good, not evil.

What is visible is a history of Christ's redeeming love breaking through to, "all God's creatures great and small."

Yes, awful things have also been done in the name of the King. But historically, the good done and lives changed (not to mention souls saved, and peace and joy received), have far-outweighed the evil done by misguided believers. Blessed are those who worship Him and touch the poor and needy because of His love. Though they have not seen the resurrected Lord face to face, yet they worship Him and serve Him.

Think of hospitals and ministries that would not exist, helps ministries such as Northwest Medical teams, Mercy Corps, Samaritan's Purse and so many more accept for faith in Christ as compassionate Lord and healer.

Phil Yancey reported that the Russians appealed to Americans at one point asking how to get their own people to respond and give aide to victims of the Chernobyl nuclear plant disaster.

Say what you will, I believe Americans reach out in compassion because of our Christian heritage.

Truth is far more than just facts. Science and math can give us facts.

Our own pop-culture indicates people know there is more than can be seen merely by our eyes. They are searching and are hungry for spiritual experience, to partake of ultimate reality. So they tattoo their bodies looking for an ultimate sense of identity and some sense of committing to that which is permanent.

Or perhaps they delve into eastern mysticism, or even into the polar opposite of the Light who is Jesus, witchcraft and dark power.

Jesus, however said, "I am the Way, Truth and Life." Look to me. What other teacher of ultimate reality has spoken so boldly?

"Come to me, I am the Truth!"

God and truth are of necessity bound together in complete reliability. If He is not truth, He is not God. C.S. Lewis said that when confronted with the astounding claims of Jesus regarding who He really is, we only have three choices. One, He was completely deluded and insane (an accusation initially believed by his own family).

Two, He knew He was not co-equal with God. His miracles came from a dark deceiving power (an accusation made by religious leaders of His own day). Or three, He is exactly who He says He is, God in the flesh.

Even the uneducated blind man who was healed by Jesus was incredulous when religious leaders interrogated Him about who had healed him. Who else but God had this kind of power?

As Lewis said, let us not glibly say that He was just a great teacher or a prophet.

He did not leave us that option!

Jesus said, "Unless you become like one of these little children you cannot enter into the kingdom."[4] Very young children are without guile and are innocently honest.

Oliver Wendell Holmes said "Pretty much all the honest truth-telling in the world is done by children." Jesus said, "make it easy for them to come to Me, do not hinder them."[5]

Often we have made His good news far too complex and burdened with the traditions of men.

Contrast this with Jesus simple promise: "You shall know the truth and the truth will set you free."[6]

Jesus knew of course that He was plowing new ground, declaring a new kingdom with a new King who would conquer hearts with His humble death on a cross. In so doing, He also was reinterpreting basic truths about His Father who had been so misrepresented.

In the opening paragraphs of the Gospel of John, the apostle declares the astounding truth that Jesus, the Word, became flesh and lived among us. This is still the greatest miracle of all God's interaction with mankind.

He became one of us. If He had not, one could say God is in His Heaven, holy and untouchable. The distance could only be reached by means of priests and sacrifices.

But now, He has come, conceived of the Holy Spirit, born and raised, tempted and tried, just as we are in this life. He became the living Word, the "Walking Truth" so we could see the loving heart of His Father.

He came to reveal who God really is as personality, not simply as the Lawgiver. His "tender commandments," as Pastor Ron Mehl calls them, had been amplified and multiplied so much that Jesus himself resisted these traditions as burdensome. He is the God who took our well- deserved punishment for sin, not like other false deities whose inventors exact unending sacrifices for insecure followers who always fear that they never can appease and satisfy. Paul states that Jesus is the face of God.[7]

Jesus illustrated to us perfectly who God always wanted us to know Him to be.

Commentators indicate that in John's gospel the word "truth" is used some twenty-five times. As we proceed, I have chosen to focus on those sayings in John that begin with, "Truly I say unto you." It is not that I think any of His other sayings are less important.

But I was interested in why He may have prefaced these certain remarks with this emphatic appeal to listen as He speaks truth.

I have apportioned the sayings into ten chapters, some of which may include more than one saying because they are linked together by the context.

In these truth statements we will explore some of the simple yet profound teachings of Jesus.

We will explore His revelation of the Father; the person and character of Christ Himself, the relationship of Father and Son and how it includes us.

We will also apply Jesus' words to our lives remembering that "grace and truth" come from Him.

We will be challenged to see how He sees us as kingdom children.

I pray that the reader will experience the profound love of our Trinitarian God for each of us, His beloved family.

Chapter I

Transformed

"I tell you the truth, no one can see the Kingdom of God unless He is born again, no one can enter the kingdom of God unless he is born of water and Spirit." John 3:3

The way into the kingdom, Jesus' predominate message, is through a transformation as radical as physical birth.

As we emerge from the womb, a warm nurturing environment of amniotic fluid totally connected to our mother by chord that links us to all that pertains to life, growth, and wholeness; we are rather violently introduced into our new environment.

We immediately long for reconnection with our mother. Anyone having witnessed this miracle will testify that it is violent, messy and traumatic for mother and child.

But oh the joy at the outcome!

So also, scripture says, all heaven erupts with joy as we are birthed into Christ's Kingdom.

Jesus says that unless we go through this radical new spiritual birthing, we cannot **see the kingdom.** Jesus taught the "gospel of the kingdom" of God. Salvation is the means by which we are transformed so we can enter this new kingdom and become one with the King. To "see," or enter this kingdom, we must be birthed into it.

There must be a complete transformation analogous to the caterpillar turning into a butterfly.

"Flesh and blood cannot inherit the kingdom."[8]

Several things are being said in regard to this birthing analogy. **One,** this is an extreme and revolutionary shift of existence that will immediately necessitate staying connected with the One who birthed us into this new kingdom.

John has already told us that now we are born not of the will of man, an earthly father and mother, rather we are spiritually born of God if we receive Christ as our Savior and Lord.

We have not seen this birth transformation in its wonderment and its full implications.

We are humble, grateful recipients of a new heredity, God's heredity. We have, if you will, a new spiritual

DNA. On the cross, He took upon Himself our propensity to sin, our "sin-nature." How awful for Him! How wonderful for us! "He became sin who knew no sin so we could become the righteousness of God in Christ Jesus."[9]

In other words, we are made right with God, who has paid the penalty for sin Himself in Christ's "substitutionary" death on the cross.

Christianity is the only religion that deals with SIN...not sins. We have died with Christ and our sin nature died in that death as we acknowledge Him as Lord and are immersed in water, buried with Him in a prophetic act that "puts to death our old sin nature".[10] We are to "put on our new self which is being renewed in the knowledge and the image of Christ,".[11]

We no longer have a slave mentality suffering under the hard ownership of sin's oppression as Israel did in Egypt.

"Our old self was crucified with Him so that the body of sin might be done away with, that we should no longer be slaves to sin—because anyone who has died has been freed from Sin."[12]

We therefore become willing servants of the One who set us free.

We have been called from darkness to light. He has made us sons and daughters of the Most High God, born of God. "No one born of God practices sin," John says[13]. Why? Because "we have the seed of God in us," we are of His seed, we make lousy sinners.

We do not want to sin, we gravitate towards righteousness. He now has put his laws, those things closest to His heart into our heart.[14]

We are not according to scripture "sinners saved by grace." We **were** sinners who have been saved by grace. Now He gives us a new name, *saints*, as we become more and more like Him. [15]

Because we love Him, we pursue and protect our Father's heart out of relationship with Him, not relationship with law.

Through the law came fear of punishment and the sober realization that we need a Savior desperately. The law was a tutor to show us how much we need a Savior from the fall of man until Christ. The sacrificial system could only deal with sins, not "sin."

The law, Paul says, with its sacrificial system, was capable of saving no one, of perfecting no one. Only through Jesus' death of full pardon, by the changing of the covenant, the former will and testament, through His death, can we now receive mercy instead of judgment, grace instead of punishment.

His offer, His gift of grace and mercy rather than punishment indeed is "good news!"

It is incredible! It is in fact hard for some to believe because it offends our human sense of earning and paying for everything.

We are born of the God whose "ways are not our ways," and thoughts have not been our thoughts. However, in His family, He is revealing His thoughts and ways to us as we can receive them, line upon line, precept upon precept. And when we really see them, we realize how radical and revolutionary they are! Yes, we are part of a prophetic community (Acts 2) called together by His Spirit to hear His heart and obey His will and to share His heart with others.

This pathway is not meant to be a solo journey. We need each other to discern the Voice of His Spirit.

We have never been here before and we need a very Personal Guide as we begin our new life. Throughout our journey we will need continual direction until we finally see Him face to face. The Holy Spirit is our Guide.

He is also like a midwife, birthing us, comforting us, reconnecting us to our Father who comprises both male and female attributes as we are placed in his arms, to hold, love and suckle us as we now feed on His word, the milk and meat of life.

In this same gospel, Jesus reveals that He is the bread from heaven imparting eternal life; that we are to partake of Him, receive Him into ourselves so that there is a dynamic fellowship: He in us, and we in Him.

God's Spirit is Personality, not an "it."

He is like an invisible umbilical cord connecting us integrally to our Parent and His Son our Savior. He promises us as we embrace them personally, and embrace their ways, that we will live in them, and have our being in them as Paul said. And initially, they, Three in One, amazing grace, abide in us!

Indeed, Trinitarian love becomes our all in all, providing all we need for life and growth in this new reality. Without God in three persons, we are lost. He, Father, Spirit and Son, is our only Guide, providing sign posts along the way, saying "This is the way, walk this way, as you turn to the right or the left."[16] So in this new kingdom, one of the highest values is to "listen." Let the church, the family of God, "have ears to hear what the Spirit says" to them.

Jesus gives us word pictures to help us understand the absolute need for connection with the Godhead. He is vine and we are His branches. How integrally we must be linked with Him.

One of my favorite analogies is the picture of those who wait upon the Lord shall rise up on the wings of an eagle, from Isaiah 40, an illustration keen in my mind as I write.

Coming home from visiting my oldest daughter and husband and our first granddaughter, we drove for several hours through the gorgeous grandeur of the Columbia River basin which divides Washington from Oregon. I was worshipping and marveling at the beautiful white puffy clouds above the deep blue river, the magnificent rock formations, and high, sheer, majestic cliffs on the Oregon side.

My wife was napping or I would have alerted her to suddenly see a magnificent bald eagle that effortlessly rose higher and higher as he caught the updrafts. He finally went so high it was as if he merged into the sun which was shining through the windshield.

What a beautiful illustration of our journey.

If we will rest in Him, we like the eagle will catch the wind of the Spirit's empowerment as we soar ever upward towards His glorious Son.

One of my favorite movies is the story of *Sea Biscuit*. In one scene where Red, the Jockey, and Sea Biscuit's trainer are training Sea Biscuit at night, with no track lights so no one can spy on them. The trainer, a wise and experienced horseman wants Red to take him around the whole course so He can get comfortable with it before the race. Red is shocked. He exclaims, "But I can't see out there."

Not only is Red blind in one eye, which was revealed earlier in the story, but now it is very dark on the track.

His trainer reassures him, "I know you can't see, but He can!" So often we can't see the track, and we fear faltering, but His Spirit can see. Jesus has been there before and was tempted in every way, tested in every way, and for our sakes was without fault or failure.

He did not falter! "He will be our Guide, hold us closely to his side" said the song writer.

"Thy word is a lamp unto our feet and a light unto our path." The Holy Spirit makes Jesus' word come alive for those who seek truth.

He also speaks in our inner person to be our guide.

Jesus initiates this call to look and listen by saying to His disciples at the very first meetings, "Come and see." Then He virtually shouts to those who heard His human voice in Palestine and those who seek Him now that they must, " Listen, Listen," "Truly, truly, verily, verily." "Listen to me, I am telling you the truth about what your life will be without me in contrast to life in me and I in you."

"I am saying life without me is slow death, you are dead men and women walking around unconnected with the source of all life, the Creator of all, Who loves you so deeply, that He sent me so you could see the King, the exact replica of His Father, and be birthed into His new Kingdom," (*my paraphrase*).

In Jerry Cook's book, *The Monday Morning Church*, He poignantly describes those without Christ as if they are walking around unplugged from the only real life support system available. Because we are afraid at this realization, we look for alternatives and are disappointed and disillusioned; so we end up using and hurting each other in our frustration. We must receive the life He offers us. There is no other alternative.

The King comes to show us who His Father really is, full of love and compassion, full of mercies that are new every morning, not desiring that any one should perish. In short, Father God is good all the time.

He enters into our reality fully incarnated in Christ, making Himself humble, vulnerable, needy, and born of a virgin.

He is **born into our reality to show us there is a new reality**, to show us what it looks like to live perfectly in this new reality. **His pure life was never meant to intimidate and shame us by reason of our failure to live up to His perfect example, but to inspire us to see what we are becoming, as we yield to His Spirit in us.**

The Kingdom-Visible and Invisible

The second thing Jesus seems to be saying is this kingdom though authored and sustained by the invisible One, has a quality that *can* be noticed, noted and experienced.

As you receive Him, you will see this Kingdom even though it is created and empowered by the invisible One. **So this kingdom is both visible and invisible, water and Spirit.** What we see are manifestations of the kingdom both in the Person of Jesus, in His disciples and in His early church, (and please Lord), in His later-day body of believers. What we see and experience in Him is light. Jesus declares He is the Light of life. Though most of us do not see Him visibly, He has given us new eyes to see into the spirit realm and new ears to hear what the Spirit is saying.

That is why Paul prays that the eyes of our heart will be kept open to the revelation of Christ and the power manifested in His resurrection and now manifested in His church…yes, the **same** power.[17] O let the church see and understand His revealed truth in these end-times! "They looked to Him and their faces were made radiant."[18] Then let us also stay in His light and "hear what the Spirit says to the churches."

"Eye has not seen, ear has not heard the wonderful things God has revealed to those who love Him, but He has revealed it, and is revealing it to us by His Spirit."[19]

Furthermore, "we have the mind of Christ."[20] His light shines through His body **which is the visible manifestation of Jesus in the earth** in this epic time as He seeks to restore all things back to His original intent for His beloved children.

The later glory however, will be even greater than the former as He restores and purifies His bride, his chosen treasure, so that she will be pure and stainless for the wedding supper of the Lamb.

A High and Noble Destiny

He does so not by fear of punishment, or by control, nor by laying down the law, but by calling us to our destiny in Him and in His kingdom. He models what we are becoming in His teachings and by His life.

"From His fullness, we have all received grace upon grace."[21] From the Only One who could justifiably condemn us, we receive mercy and the challenge to "sin no more," so we can live up to the destiny to which He has called us.

"All creation is waiting with eager expectation for the sons (and daughters) of God to be revealed."[22]

We must embrace who the Lord says we are, the righteousness of God in Christ Jesus, rather than embracing some false humility that says we are junk.

We are lights filled with His light, the city of God, to be lifted high so all men can see the transformation into His likeness that He, by His Spirit, is working in His children.

How we relate to this invisible realm of light has everything to do with fruitfulness or sadly to barrenness in our lives. Come into the light, more succinctly, come to the One who is Light and Life, invisible—yet visible to your spiritual eyes. Jesus says even now, "**We speak of what we know, what we have seen."**

No one has gone into heaven except the One who came from heaven. He must be lifted up, this Son of Man, so everyone who believes may have eternal life."[23] The Hebrew concept of knowledge, of knowing is never focused on knowledge without experience.

Experience is the foundation of knowledge. The Kingdom is then knowable, and notable, that is, experiential, visible through our new sanctified spiritual eyes even though empowered by the invisible wind of the Spirit.

We are ambassadors of the King implanted within darkness so that we will "arise and shine for the glory of the Lord is on us"[24] and in us!

Would that we would live and move and have our being in the glory of the manifest presence of the Lord so fully that we, like the priests at Solomon's temple dedication, would be totally overwhelmed with His presence.

The Wind of the Spirit Produces Fruit

The signs of the wind of the Spirit are everywhere if one looks with spiritual eyes.

What God has done and is still doing can be understood and embraced with gratitude and expectancy. The branches of the vine are bearing fruit, more fruit, and much fruit as the wind of God's Spirit blows upon them.

The Kingdom manifests light and life as God's kids reach out to the poor and needy, as Mercy Core, Samaritan's Purse, Northwest Medical Teams, and other ministries are on site with Christ's love and resources helping the victims of calamitous upheaval.

Signs and wonders are confirming the word through Roland and Heidi Baker in Zimbabwe as they feed multitudes of poor and pray for the sick. Thousands accept Christ and receive healings after seeing the gospel in the *Jesus Film* shown by Campus Crusade all around the world.

But just as notably, the love of Christ is poured out in a simple plate of cookies for ones neighbor, or a hospice worker helping usher one into Christ's very presence.

And never forget, all heaven throws a party every time there is a new birth into the kingdom, miracle of all miracles!

But these humble and "ordinary" acts of love in no way diminish the truth that "signs and wonders are to follow" believers wherever Christ is proclaimed.

Remember, we are born of the water, and the Spirit. The Spirit portions out various gifts as needed and necessary today, even as they were in the early church. Are there any who would not want the *fullness* of the Spirit that the Apostle Paul declares as Christ's goal for His church in the letter to the Ephesians?

Would anyone not desire Jesus to breathe on us His Holy Spirit even as He did His apostles after His resurrection?

How are our lives a demonstration of the Spirit's empowerment?

Where is that whimsical, often surprising aspect of the beautiful Holy Spirit's ministry?

Where is the Lord God of Elijah today in our ministries?

Jesus said, "Go preach the good news to all nations, and these signs will accompany those who believe. In my name they will drive out demons, they will speak in new tongues, they will pick up snakes with their hands and when they drink deadly poison it will not hurt them at all; and they will place their hands on sick people, and they will get well."[25] James said call the elders, anoint with oil and the prayer of faith will raise up the sick.

The early church did all the same miracles Jesus did and more, because they could be in so many more places having each been filled with His Spirit. "Greater things shall you do," is still a challenge to today's church to be all and embrace all that the Spirit desires to do in the earth.

Contenders for the faith may not always get the outcome they desire, but we still obey the mandate to lay hands on the sick and they will recover. The truth is that we do not stop praying and believing for healing because some do not get healed anymore than we stop preaching the word because some do not get saved! The mandate is still there.

"These signs and wonders shall follow!"

Every time the church gathers there should be a "sighting," a manifestation of the Spirit's presence and activity like the bursting forth of a whale breaching the surface of the water.

"There she blows! Spirit sighting! Spirit sighting!"

How will the Spirit manifest Himself today in our presence? "Come and see you who are born of water and Spirit."

Celebrate the results of the fresh wind of the Spirit in your midst. "Blessed are those who hunger and thirst after righteousness for they shall be filled."[26] His promise—to fill us—our responsibility—to stay hungry and thirsty for His presence!

Teach us, dear Lord, to walk in the fullness of your glory. Amen!

Chapter II

Like Father, Like Son

*"**I tell you the truth,** the Son can do nothing by Himself. He can only do what He sees His Father doing because whatever the Father does the Son does also." John 5:19*

In the previous chapter we learned that to be a part of Christ's kingdom, we must enter into a radical birthing process authored by the Holy Spirit. He then becomes our guide in this spiritual journey. Therefore, listening is of the highest priority in His kingdom.

If, in fact, we are listening our lives will exhibit corresponding fruit as we are continually filled with His Spirit. All this speaks of a high level of intimacy and oneness with the Godhead. This oneness is our highest priority as exemplified in the life of Christ.

He said He could only do whatever the Father was doing.

The Religious leaders sought to persecute Him since His response to their question of why he healed the paralytic at the Pool of Bethesda was: "My Father is always at His work to this very day, and I too am working," (5:16). For this reason they sought to kill him since he made himself to be equal with God.

This paralytic man was then rebuked by the religious authorities who saw him walking with his mat. According to them, carrying the mat upon which he lay every day was forbidden by the law, since this day was the Sabbath. But the man who healed him said, "Get up and pick up your mat and walk."

He had been waiting at this pool as a paralytic for many years to get in the water as it was stirred by an angel of the Lord (as some manuscripts report). But someone always beat him to it. The religious authorities asked for the name of the one who had told him to pick up his mat and walk, but he did not know who it was. Jesus had slipped away from the crowds (I love that) and later came to the healed man in the temple. He told him to stop sinning "or something worse may happen."

The healed man, of course, told the Jews it was Jesus who had made him well.

I find several aspects of this story amazing. First, the sensitivity of the Lord Jesus to focus on this one who was obviously hopeless, perhaps angry, or even bitter at his lot in life.

Yet, he kept coming to this place to see if perhaps this was the day. We have to admire his perseverance.

Jesus asked one of His classic questions, "Do you want to get well?"

Of course he did!

Obviously Jesus knew his heart and challenged him to shift His focus to gaze into the eyes of the One who created the waters which fed the spring and filled the pool, to hear God speak through His Son, "Get up! Pick up your mat and walk."

Keep Your Eyes on Jesus, Not the Old Packaging

What a magnificent illustration of Jesus interrupting the type of thinking that put God in a box (in this case a pool). Jesus is saying in effect, "Listen to me! Your healing is in me, in the Person of God the Son. I now heal you because God is always working for His beloved."

Often the packaging of what we are looking for may have changed since last we went looking.

My wife says we men have a missing gene when it comes to finding things in the house!

I was explaining that because I was looking for the old packaging, I did not see the item for which I was searching (it was rather well hidden at the back corner of the refrigerator).

But here is the point: Perspective often results in tunnel vision. (In a recent study, it was concluded that men because of their hunter gather-genes physiologically do not have as wide a span of eyesight as women. They are better at single focus sighting and pursuit, it seems). Anyway, that's my story and I'm sticking to it!

The nation of Israel is a classic example of looking for different packaging than what came to them as the Messiah. Sadly, they rejected the One standing right in front of them, healing their diseases and delivering those possessed by evil spirits, just as Isaiah had prophesied.[27]

Jesus indicted them by saying "you search the scriptures daily" but do not recognize the author of those scriptures standing in front of your face!

How then are we as modern day believers "missing" the ministry of the Messiah by reason of our own preconceptions?

How have we missed the still small voice as did Elijah did, expecting Him to come spectacularly again in the wind, or fire, or earthquake like He has done before.

Or just the opposite, how have we rejected the spectacular; because, that is not the way He has worked in the past? How often have we missed His coming to us in a brother or sister who may have challenged our preconceptions, but to whom we gave no thought of credibility, and no power to help us shift our paradigm? How often have we missed an opportunity of gratitude for an answer from God by labeling the event just coincidence?

Trophies of Healing

Jesus said, "Get up! Pick up your mat and walk!" His mat was the makeshift mattress upon which he lay every day illustrating to everyone who walked by that he was paralyzed. Now he has been loosed from his paralysis, Jesus says, pick up that symbol of your paralysis and carry it with you so everyone can see your liberation.

What had imprisoned him became a symbol of his release, a trophy of His healing.

Jesus found him later in the temple, perhaps giving thanks, perhaps showing himself to the priests as was required by law.

Everyone must have known who he was, including the priests. Yet here he stands, as a normal functioning man, holding the item upon which he was imprisoned for so many years. It is astounding that the religious authorities would not even take one moment to rejoice with the precious man who had been set free from paralysis after 38 years!

I heard of a church where the youth pastor was miraculously healed of partial paralysis on his right side. He walked with a debilitating limp and was unable to use his right arm.

The congregation prayed for him publically.

About a week later he shared his testimony of total healing. Pastor shared that while many rejoiced; over thirty families wrote letters and e-mails saying they were leaving because this did not fit with their theology!

They would not rejoice that one who was in bondage was set free!

But before we get too caught up in judgment of the priests who rebuked him, what thing or person or system of thought would Jesus want to interrupt in *our grid* and say, "shift your eyes to me, look at me, I am your Savior, Healer, Deliver, Provider, and Comforter?

Into what religious boxes have your restrictive mindsets delegated the Lord?

He died to break you out of any kind of religious box that could block the blessings He desires to impart to you. But, you may object; "Who can stop the Lord from doing what He wants?"

Consider this kind of a belief statement; "You can't do that Jesus, this is the only authorized way. I am waiting for you to do it this way."

Church historians tell us that every new move of God has been resisted by the previous move of God by reason of these very mindsets.

How have we bought into a system of thought that basically is designed by men to explain away Jesus' teaching when we do not see the results we desire?

"Well, He really did not mean that we could speak to a mountain expecting it to be miraculously moved."

"I mean, if God wants to heal or provide miraculously on His own—He is God. But we can't really pray and expect that."

If not, then what do we have in covenant with the Lord that distinguishes us from an unbeliever? Even they experience God's common grace. Is there not something of special grace that belongs to the Lord's sons and daughters in His Kingdom?

What would Jesus tell you to pick up and carry in order to demonstrate that he has freed you from a **prison of limitations?**

What is the thing upon which you rested to illustrate your bondage? What has been the symbol of your imprisonment?

A co-dependent relationship with someone, a "drug of choice" either chemical, emotional, even pseudo spiritual that you have "lain upon" for years, searching for freedom. It has become comfortable.

You identify with it and identify yourself by it.

Jesus says "Get Up!"

Hear Jesus saying, "look at me, listen to me, **I tell you the truth**. Here—in me you will find real freedom." "Hear my word of truth which would set you free indeed.

Take the first step, receive authentic freedom." "Move from this place where you are stuck to this new kingdom space, inhabited by Me, as you embrace Me, the Life-Giver and Deliverer."

"Take up your mat and walk." We must not be afraid to talk about the weaknesses from which Jesus is liberating us to those who may need our encouragement.

Certainly, we would rather no one know our "stuff." But just think of how many have found hope in hearing those who have "taken up their mat," share their testimony of true freedom found in Jesus. This is not a trophy to be hung on the wall. Rather, it is our opportunity to be transparent with others and share how our weaknesses give Christ space to strengthen and perfect us.

Back to the story, Jesus takes it a step higher.

"Yes, to your amazement He (the Father) will show Him (the Son) even greater things."

"For just as the Father raises the dead and gives them life, even so the Son gives life to whom He is pleased to give it."[28]

In other words, "You ain't seen nothin' yet!"

"**I tell you the truth,** whoever hears my word and believes Him who sent me has eternal life and **will not be condemned; he has crossed over from death to life**."

"The time is coming and now has come, when the dead will hear the voice of the Son of God and those who hear will live."[29]

"Has come" is a "point in time" expression, meaning at this point in time, this new reality has begun! We must lay hold of the liberating words of Jesus, the Word, and take up our mat and walk.

Doing What Father is Doing

The first thing I noted was Jesus sensitivity to reach out to this one in such desperate need of healing. Secondly, I also am amazed at Jesus' humility. Though He is God in the flesh, having laid aside His glory (not His divinity), He is totally submissive to His Father's will and purpose in His earthly mission.

How different would my own life and ministry be if I lived out that true-north principle?

I pray for that kind of relationship and sensitivity to the Lord, but often fall very short of "doing what the Father is doing."

I don't think it is usually pride or lack of obedience. Rather, I often lack the confidence that I am hearing Him clearly.

The Way We See Ourselves

But not so fast partner! There is a flip side of pride, not the braggadocios, "I am the best thing since peanut butter" side, but the "I am just a sinner saved by grace" or the, "who am I?" side.

We are really saying, "**I am a special case.**" "Really, you should choose someone else Lord."

This is the false humility with which I and others have struggled.

I am finally beginning to know that "I am confident in this very thing: that He who began a good work will bring it to completion."[30]

I am not a sinner anymore, I am saved by grace. I am a "saint" whose old man, (sin nature), was crucified on the cross with Christ. My old man, my sin nature if you will, was buried with Him into death in the Jordan River of baptism, and I am a new creature in His kingdom! Sin is no longer my master, Jesus is my Master in Whom I am now a willing slave, but with Whom I am now a brother and a friend by His reckoning.

When I do sin, He is there to receive my repentance with love and mercy. He is not into punishment for His kids. He bore our punishment at Calvary. He is my advocate John later says in his letter to the churches.

Help me Lord to reckon these truths as **the truth.**

Why is this understanding so important? "As a man thinks in his heart, so is He!"[31] Someone has said, "if you call someone a sinner enough times, he is going to sin because that is the way he sees himself."

"Well, I am no saint you know." Really, God says as His child, you are! The Apostle Paul did not write to the sinners at Ephesus and Corinth, he wrote to the saints and said that is what they were called to be saints.[32]

So as a saint, the Lord has given us new ears, new eyes, and a new heart into which He has written the concerns of His heart. He has given His Holy Spirit to abide within us so we can be led, to "do what Father is doing" just as Jesus did. You see "the righteous are bold as a lion; the wicked flee when no one is chasing them."[33] Daniel says "Those who know their God will do great exploits"[34] (*Grrrreat! Sorry, couldn't resist*!)

Remember, Jesus said we would do even greater things than He did after He returned to glory and poured out His Spirit.

"The Father loves His Son and shows Him all that He does."[35]

Here is the encouragement, that because we are in Christ who has been loved since before time, and since God says He loves us and proves that love by sending Jesus to restore fellowship with the Father; He will also show us all that he is doing, so we can be co-laborers with His Spirit.

How fruitful I would be in my life if I acknowledge, not just that I can do nothing without the Father, but that I **can do** only that which I see him doing. "I can do all things through Christ who strengthens me."[36]

But you may say, Jesus was special, the "Only Begotten Son" sent from God to reconcile the world to Himself. The Apostle Paul says that we have been given the ministry of reconciliation; that we are sent as ambassadors of Christ. Jesus' sheep know His voice. "Moreover, they will never follow a stranger."[37] Perhaps nothing is "stranger" than us trying to follow **our own voice** instead of waiting to hear Father's voice, doing what we think best individually and as a church, but all the while operating out of a world system mindset in regards to how we govern our churches, like a business, how we approach ministry, by doing programs, how we raise funds, by hiring some slick promoter as a professional fundraiser and so on *ad nauseum*.

What, pray tell, would happen if we stopped, and listened intently to the heart of the Father, then began to do "the work He is always doing."

"He (the Father) will show Him (the Son) even greater things than these."[38] "Whoever hears my word and believes him who sent me has eternal life and will not be condemned; he has crossed over from death to life."[39]

"If we are "in Christ" as the Apostle Paul says we are, then can we not lay hold of this promise of greater things? Christ is also "in us." "He is the hope of (present and future) glory."

Father, let us hear Your voice and that of Your Son, our Savior, so we may be about Your business even as He was and is: the business of life, that as we hear Your voice, we become dispensers of Your life.

By the Spirit's empowerment, help us live lives that declare to those who are the walking dead, those who have lost hope and are paralyzed waiting for the waters to stir, hear the voice of the Lover of your soul. Arise take your mat and walk.

Chapter III

That Which Really Satisfies

*"**I tell you the truth;** you seek me, not because you saw signs, but because you ate your fill of the loaves. Do not labor for food which perishes, but for the food with endures to eternal life which the Son of man will give you; for on Him has God the Father set His seal." John 6:30*

Jesus is trying to lift the gaze of the people higher than temporal things to that which is eternal, "food which endures to eternal life."

He states that if they had come because of the signs, that would indicate some kind of faith, though not the highest kind. But sadly, all their focus was on the possibility of full stomachs. The day before, after feeding five thousand with five loaves and two fish, He perceived that they were about to come and take Him by force to make him king.

So he escaped up to a mountain to be alone. (You have to love His humility and ability to stay the course). He must cause them to lift their vision higher than food for a meal, or even miraculous food from a king.

He is leading up to the revelation that He is the Bread of Eternal Life, the nature of which is eternally satisfying.

Many who had been fed now sought Him on the other side of the Sea of Galilee in Capernaum.

This is the place where He and His disciples had been miraculously transported after taking Jesus, who was strolling on the water, into their boat.

After Jesus tells them to labor for eternal food given to them by the Son of Man, the Jews ask Him, "What must we do, to be doing the works of God?" Probably expecting a long list similar to what the local priests and Pharisees were teaching, they might have been shocked at the brevity of Christ's answer.

He said, "This is the work of God: that you believe in Him whom He has sent."

We get the sense that they are not sincere in their question regarding the works of God.

Their response to Jesus' pronouncement is to allude to the manna Moses provided.

"Show us some sign that we should believe you are sent of God. Moses gave us manna in the wilderness. What will you do?"[40]

But Jesus immediately corrected their tradition saying, "**I tell you the truth;** it was not Moses, but God who gives true bread from heaven, it comes down from heaven and gives life to the world."[41] Their response: "Lord, give us this bread always." Then Jesus gets to the core of this encounter by once again lifting their focus from their bellies to their state of being. "**I am the bread of life**; whoever comes to me shall not hunger, whoever believes in me shall never thirst."

Jesus herein gives the first of many "I Am" statements, all self-disclosures that have become familiar to us regarding His nature and character, each one pregnant with revelation of the saving work of God manifested in Christ.

Later in this discourse he declares that whoever eats of this "Living Bread" which has come down from heaven, will live forever. "He who believes has eternal life."[42]

This comes after they have indirectly accused Him of lying by saying, "what does He mean He's come from heaven? This is Joseph and Mary's boy right?"

He reassures them that, in fact, He alone has seen the Father, evidence of being sent by Him.

As if that was not revolutionary enough, now He really creates a hubbub by further stating that His flesh is the bread that He will offer up for the salvation of the world. Of course, they began to dispute His statement among themselves saying, "How can this man give His flesh to eat?"

You can feel it coming, at least if you live on this side of the cross. But even his disciples are shocked and some appalled at His next statement.

"**I tell you the truth**, unless you eat the flesh and drink the blood of the Son of man you have no life in you; He who eats my flesh and drinks my blood will have eternal life and I will raise him up on the last day."[43]

Most except for the twelve apparently, thought, "Now He has gone too far!"

They were offended. Rightly so, Jews were trained to never drink blood as pagans did, and to never eat any kind of meat without totally draining the blood.

Life is in the blood!

Take the blood out of a living thing with perfectly functioning organs, and you have taken away the life force. Blood was what atoned for the sins of the people in the Old Covenant. But that is exactly it, isn't it?

Jesus is explaining to them how His pummeled flesh and His shed blood will be the propitiation, that is , the awful and wonderful price paid to appease the just judgment of God for all men for all time, once and for all!

He really does not even try to soften the offense of this statement. The cross event will not be softened for Him! That is, not to say, His statement is vindictive, no, He simply tells the unadorned, unvarnished truth, knowing many who will now turn away were there for wrong reasons, temporal reasons.

Jesus is about as un-Madison Avenue as you can get. No one taught Him basic church growth techniques about comfort zones or being user-friendly. He probably offended or at least confused even the chosen apostles.

"After this, many of his disciples drew back from Him and no longer went with Him.

He even asked the twelve remaining, "Are you going to leave me also?" But Peter got it.

"Lord where else would we go; you have the words of eternal life."⁴⁴ Peter is saying as it were, "When you speak and when I observe the way you live, something resonates deep within me in a manner I could only dream about, until I encountered you." You are what I always had longed for God to be.

You are "the Holy One," an expression only used twice in the New Testament. Peter is saying by revelation of the Father, you are God in the flesh.

"You are the Christ the Son of the Living God" is the Synoptic Gospels' record of Peter's breakthrough confession. To Peter, hearing the words of Jesus called him to his real destiny, far from fishing for fish, he would be fishing for men! "You are Simon. But you shall be called Peter, the Rock."

Furthermore, it would be upon his leadership and this very confession that Jesus would build His church, the gathering of His followers.

Don't you love that about Jesus?

He sees life from the end, knowing who we are to become in His kingdom, and calls us into that destiny.

The truth grows from a seed to a tree of life within this chapter's revelation of Jesus.

To have life, eternal life, we must partake of Him in a "once for all action," receiving Him as Lord and Savior bringing eternal life; but we receive also in a continuous action as we constantly long for more "Spirit and Life."

He uses the word "abides" speaking of **a mutual continuous partaking and interaction**, more than a fleeting contact of His communion with us. He is the Heavenly Bread of Life come down from the Father to offer His very body to buy men back from separation from the Father, a Father who so longs for fellowship with His children.

Here Jesus declares that this offer of fellowship is eternal.

From this side of the cross it is so much easier not to be shocked by Jesus' cannibalistic saying because we now understand the analogy He is making. Jesus may not be referring directly to the New Covenant meal in this instance as some commentators have concluded, since he uses the word "flesh" rather than "body," the usual word for the covenant meal. If this does not refer to the covenant meal, that only makes His statement that we must eat his flesh and drink His blood even more astonishing and specific. It is a call to intimacy.

Jesus had said to his disciples after ministering to the woman at the well in John 4, "I have food you do not know about...doing my Fathers will." Remarkably, here **He is the food** that gives eternal life. The Greek word "to eat" of His flesh speaks of joyful, noisy, crunching, chomping, and delight.

That is how we take Him into our hearts and souls; we partake of the bread of heaven in receiving Him as the Word in alone times in sweet intimacy. We do so also in communion the bread and fruit of the vine representing His blood. Though we do not embrace the doctrine of transubstantiation (partaking the actual blood and flesh in communion), we

Protestants I fear make far too little of the spiritual transition that happens as we do partake.

These potent word pictures are invitations to fully partake of His Personhood as He partakes of ours.

Before his crucifixion, Jesus initiates His New Covenant meal wherein we partake of His body and blood, the bread and wine of the Lord's Supper. This holy meal feeds us with life eternal because of what these sacramental symbols mean, because of what was accomplished in Christ's death, burial and resurrection.

Lifting our gaze higher, to God's motive for redemption, we must realize that God's salvation **is for an even higher passion, His passion to be one with His children** and establish a kingdom through which that oneness is wholly possible. He tore down the wall that separated us from Him by reason of sin and rebellion.

"God so loved...He gave..."[45]

Jesus with that same Father heart so loved, that He offered Himself.

If we could only grasp His call to intimacy in all of this, what a difference it would make in our own peace of mind, and as a result, in "peace on earth and good will to men."

The Jews asked about "doing" for God. Jesus, however was talking about "being," partaking of Him, believing in Him, living in a state of hunger and thirst for Him, yet finally content in Him. He invites perpetual longing for more of Heaven's Bread. This Bread will never disappoint and will never spoil. It is true Bread, true in every way.

In fact, it cannot be anything other than true, for it is the embodiment of truth. In this Bread's presence is fullness of joy!

When Jesus asked if the disciples were also going to leave Him in John 6:67, Peter's answer struck the bull's eye.

"Where else could we go Lord? You have the words of life! We believe and know that You are the Holy One of God." It is in partaking joyfully of Jesus, the Bread of Life that we find life. He declares that, "He who eats Me, will live because of Me."[46]

This is a continuous action verb. Though we have eaten, received Him into our spirit and soul, having been drawn by the Father's initiative to be "born again," we continually feed on the Bread of Life for sustenance.

We drink from the fountain of life, are finally satisfied, and yet paradoxically desire more and more.[47]

Sadly, even as believers who have tasted and seen His goodness, we are easily distracted and go looking elsewhere. We look for satisfaction but, "Can't get no satisfaction."

"We've tried and we've tried," more entertainment, more recreation, more stuff, new relationships, more status, more power, more influence, bigger ministries. But our hearts still ache for real Bread from Heaven. Truly, "all that glitters ain't gold."

It never delivers anything of eternal value and ultimately disappoints, leading to disillusionment and despair.

It is just fool's gold.

Why do our hearts roam? Perhaps, deep down we think the Lord really doesn't like us, so we pull away. Perhaps we still carry a lot of baggage, like rejection, or fear, or inability to trust. We believe the lie from hell that these issues with which we grapple somehow disqualify us from intimacy with the Godhead.

Or, perhaps C.S. Lewis' great observation is the real truth, that seeking pleasure is not the problem. The real problem is that we tend to seek lesser pleasures, neglecting the highest pleasure of all, God's precious presence.

Hear the invitation of Jesus to eat His flesh and drink His blood as the call to intimacy that it truly is. Partake of Him, eat His words, chew on them, swallow and digest them into yourself and revel in the life they impart.

 Drink His blood in the sense that you truly "take in" what is being made available at the table of the Lord by reason of His shed blood at Calvary. Do not be one who does not "discern the body" that is, who does not really understand what was purchased for them by their beautiful Savior's shed blood. Saint Paul said some are sick and have died prematurely because they have not understood the blessings resident within the bread and cup of Christ.[48]

Daily in His presence drink in His life force as it were. He is the Fountain of Life.

Become partakers of His divine nature as Peter later says in his letters to the churches.

Eat of the bread of His words, drink from the fruit of His lips, embrace and receive the implanted word, the "*sperma*" of God, (one of the Greek words for word).

Celebrate oneness with the One who is our wisdom, righteousness, sanctification, and redemption.[49] The fruit of this union will be love, joy, peace, patience, kindness, goodness, faithfulness, gentleness, and self control.[50] These are matters of the heart. They come from seeking and coming to know the Father's heart, those things that are important to Him.

One cannot have a relationship with the rules, well, at least not happily!

Sadly that is the extent of some people's spirituality. And most in this boat are sinking in the storms of life. You cannot find comfort and encouragement in laws and rules when compared to the comfort offered in the Person of the Holy Spirit.

Moses' ministry is mentioned several times in this discussion about the bread of life.

He truly is one of the greats. But in this discourse, **Jesus points them to the real source of Moses' greatness: the presence of his God.** Moses at one point is told to go to the Promise Land and God would send an angel to accompany them. Most of us would have probably been delighted with that arrangement, but not Moses. He tests the limits of His intimacy with God by saying that if God is not going with him, he is not going.

The Lord honors His request, saying that Moses has found favor in His eyes. Here the favor of the Lord is defined as **His presence**.

Moses questions, "How will the people know that I and we as a people have found favor unless your Presence go with us?"

God promises His presence and rest will go with Moses and His people. O how we need that same mindset today as contemporary believers!

From this story we learn how much Moses valued His intimacy with God and how any power he wielded was simply as an instrument in God's hands. Meekness truly was displayed in Moses' life and leadership. God called him the meekest man alive.

He understood the priority of God's presence permeating every aspect of His life and leadership. Meekness is dependence on God's presence and consequently, his authority and power. Look what God was able to do with twelve ordinary men who were called and empowered into their destiny by spending time with Jesus. "And they shall be taught by God."[51]

So "draw near" and "do not shrink back" warns the author of Hebrews.

We please the Lord by partaking of Him. Notice that there is no list of commandments in this context because they are written on our hearts already by reason of this new covenant heart we have all been given. (Read Ezekiel, Jeremiah. Hebrews) we draw near to a Person, the Person of God the Father and His Son our Savior in and through His Holy Spirit. He has "made a new and living way opened to us through the curtain, that is, His body."[52]

This speaks of the curtain separating the worshipers in the temple from the Ark of Covenant, where the Mercy Seat, the presence of God manifested.

But He became the entry way into the presence of the Father by His body having been broken for us at the cross. The curtain was torn open signifying that now "whosoever" may come into His very presence through Christ. "We can boldly come to Father God and find grace and mercy in time of need."[53] It was Jesus' driving mission to "show us the Father."

At every step of His ministry He is revealing who God wants us to know He actually is. Later in His letters to the churches, John the beloved disciple states what Jesus showed us by His life, that "God is love." Jesus is sent and comes to earth out of eternal love for His family.

What we learn is that once we are in His presence, His magnificent love so supersedes our need, that it pales in comparison. It is not nearly so important. And when we feel no urgent need, we are then able to bask in His love and companionship because He, in fact, wants to be with us more than we with Him!

Don't get me wrong, He wants to bless. But as the intercessory song "Open Up the Sky" pleads, "We don't want blessings we want You!"[54]

We learn that we want Him more than those things He is able to provide.

Yet, He will bless because that is Who He is. "In His presence is fullness of joy, at His right hand, pleasures forever more."[55]

To believe *is* the work, Jesus says. We are to believe "that He is and that He is a rewarder of those who diligently seek Him."

We must come in trust that he will love and bless not hurt us. Jesus said, "if we have seen Him we have seen the Father."[56] The letter to the Hebrews begins by saying Jesus is the exact image of God the Father.

Jesus did not go around making people sick to teach them a lesson. He did not break a leg or arm to teach perseverance any more than we would do so to our children. He inflicted no emotional trauma on those who came to him, unless telling the truth in love is considered traumatic. On the contrary, He imparted peace never before known on earth.

He did not oppress, He delivered the oppressed.

Unlike the religious teachers of the day He did not pile heavy religious burdens upon people. Instead He offered liberating relationship with unfathomable love.

In Jesus' face resides "the knowledge of the glory of God."[57] If we spend time with Him, we will come away radiant in the knowledge of who the Father really is through our own experience guided by His Spirit.

We will come to know Him as the Bread of life, the "Manna" of Heaven, the only real contentment and satisfaction. Just like Israel, we come every morning for "Manna," the sustenance we need for the day, understanding that He is abiding in us, yet longing for more of His presence.

Keep in mind that these nutrients are growing us into the likeness of Christ so that we will become eternally compatible. As we yield to His Spirit, we will look and sound more and more like Him. Fruitfulness will be the result of abiding in the vine.[58]

 I grew up singing a hymn that was a simple prayer for more of Jesus,"Bread of Heaven, feed me till I want no more." May that be all our prayers as well as we receive grace for each moment of each day.

Chapter IV

Ever Increasing Light

"He who sent me is true, and I declare to the world what I have heard from Him." (John 8:26)

This discourse opens (in verse 12) with Jesus describing Himself as the "Light of the World." Of course, reading this story from our side of the cross, we who believe bask in the light of His saving, sustaining, and life-giving light. But to those hearing this for the first time, it was fresh revelation which brought a totally new vision of who God wanted them to be in His new kingdom.

He truly became the Light of Life for those who embraced Him as light. John says in his prologue that to those who believed, He gave the power to become sons and daughters of God. But others could not receive this new illuminating revelation.

Because of their religious mindsets, their hearts became more and more resistant to Jesus and Who He really is and was.

Sadly, they were unknowingly serving the dark lord, the enemy of truth. Outside of Christ Jesus, there is only darkness masquerading as light, where the blind lead the blind.

"Whoever follows the Light, will not walk in darkness." What is darkness? Jesus says He is "from above; they are from below and will die in their sins unless they believe" He is who He says He is, God the Son.

These verses record a lot of bantering back and forth before He reaches the climax in verse 58. As we read along, the light gets brighter and brighter as Jesus raises the level of light step by step.

However, before He astonishes them and shatters their religious preconceptions, they have quite a "who's your daddy?" conversation in which Jesus squarely confronts their resistance to "the Truth."

He declares three times in this interaction with religious leaders, "Truly, truly," or as we would say, "listen to me, I am telling you the truth."

This conversation is a primer on the dangers of religion without relationship.

Religion is man's self-reliant effort to make himself right with God. First of all, they had second-hand truth, *previous revelation*. Current revelation was standing right in front of their eyes but they were blinded by their own false security, claiming that because they were sons of Abraham, "the chosen," following the law and oral traditions of the rabbi's, they did not need whatever light Jesus was offering! They accuse Him of bragging on Himself, being His own "witness," so Jesus takes on that theme and says even in your own courts of law, two witnesses are sufficient. "I bear witness to Myself, and my Father who sent Me also bears witness."

In His mind, what else could be necessary?

They reply, where is your father? The truth is they were really asking "Who is your father?" They are starting to question his legitimacy and will even imply that He is a son of fornication while they are sons of Abraham, (41). Astounding, the arrogance of religious self-righteousness.

Jesus then pinpoints the problem with religion of any kind. It is bereft of relationship. "If you knew Me, you would know My Father also." He really is saying the reverse as well. If you really were sons of Abraham, you would know Abraham's Father and not be trying to kill the One Abraham longed to see, the one prefigured on Mount Mariah when God provided the substitutionary sacrifice in a bush. Abraham had been willing to give His son, his only son, at God's command. Now the sacrificial Lamb of God stands before the sons of Abraham.

God has provided just as Abraham had prophetically declared. But they are blinded by their own religious darkness and resistance to the light.

The religious spirit is difficult to expose because those controlled by it think they are doing right.

The primary response Jesus requires is "to believe." "I am He," was His response when they asked, "Who are you?" But it is obvious they really did not what to know unless it provided more ammunition by which they could justify the murder found in their religious hearts. He had told them all along who He was. He had demonstrated that He was filled with God's omnipotence.

He had turned water into the best wine ever; He had restored the sight of the one born blind; He had healed the official's son from a distance; He had fed over five thousand people by multiplying the loaves and fishes.

If that were not enough, the only Righteous One who has every right to condemn a woman caught in adultery...instead forgives and challenges her to fulfill her destiny.

The one who sent Jesus is "true" and Jesus declares to them what His Father, with whom He has been in audience, has revealed.

But they do not understand that He speaks of the heavenly Father who Jesus "always pleases."

Thankfully, many within earshot of this continued revelation of light actually do believe.

To those Jesus says, **"If you continue in My word, you are truly My disciples, and you will know the truth and the truth will set you free."**[59] But the religious authorities respond with another remarkable counter argument revealing their deception.

"We have no need of being set free; we have never been in bondage to anyone."

Amazing! It would seem that they have forgotten their own history, how having been delivered from the bondage of Egypt (a type of sin), they were set free to go and worship the only true God, the "I Am" who empowered Moses as their deliverer.

Along with a virtual chain of captivities due to apostasy, they are now under Roman occupation!

How deceptive this religious spirit that substitutes lists of ritual for relationship.

Over and over God restored a remnant by His mercy as they sadly repeated this process until they were so dispassionate towards God's prophetic call to repent that there had been no prophetic voice for hundreds of years until...now?

John the Baptist recently came on the scene. He prepared the way for the Truth to be received. In God's love, He was making His chosen One very clear to the chosen ones.

The Baptist may have preached to as many as two million some say. His message: "Repent for the kingdom is at hand." "Messiah is coming, get ready." And now He has come. John must decrease, the Truth must increase. Truth has come to dwell with men as a man.

Truth is a person, not a system of thought, not a list of do's and don'ts, a wonderful, marvelous Person, the "Desire of the nations."

Knowing Him, receiving Him, taking His word as absolutely true and acting upon it, will in fact set you free.

His own Spirit, the Holy Spirit which He breathed upon the Apostles post resurrection, is called the "Spirit of Truth," the Counselor, the Comforter." He guides us into all truth and reminds us of all that the Truth, Who is Jesus, has said and is saying still to those who have "ears to hear."

Now the One for whom John the Baptist prepared the way stands before them: the Way, the Truth and the Life, the Manna from heaven, "The Light," but they cannot see Him.

They are blind to Him. Not only does religion keep one in bondage, it deceives one into thinking that bondage is freedom!

Religion is a deceptive form of bondage, making a list and checking it twice in order to earn God's good graces. It promises what it cannot deliver. Jesus elsewhere says that the blind lead the blind, the bound lead others into bondage, all the while calling it freedom!

Jesus now nails it down more precisely by saying, **"Truly, truly, I say unto you, everyone who commits sin is a slave to sin."** [60]

He has come to deliver us from that "sin-slavery," not just our individual sins, but our sin nature, our human condition, the DNA that causes us to chose sin even when we do not want to. But that is exactly what focusing on rule-keeping does, Saint Paul teaches; it stirs up the desire to raid the cookie jar when Mom says not to.

God's law, though righteous, cannot solve the sin-nature issue.

It simply reminds us over and over again that we are failures and have no hope of living up to His perfect standard. The sacrifices have been offered, sins rolled forward another year, but we walked away unchanged! It was never meant to deliver nor can it transform.

It only was meant to bring order with boundaries important to God's heart and to reveal God's purity. Later in Paul's letter to the Galatians, in the, "Magna Charta" of the gospel, Paul states that while the law is good, it was meant to tutor us into the realization that our only answer is a "Deliverer" like Moses. Jesus willingly became a pure spotless Passover Lamb, perfect God and perfect man, to once and for all deliver us from our sin nature. He delivered us from the bondage of Egypt, just as the Hebrews were delivered, and lead us to the land of promise...the Kingdom of God.

But those caught in their deception cannot receive Jesus' Word because they are doing the works of their father, the devil, the direct antithesis of Jesus doing His Father's work.

Like Saul the persecutor of the early church, they believed they were acting on God's behalf, guarding the truth. But murder is not of God's Spirit, even for religious reasons, especially for religious reasons.

What an oxymoron, murder in the name of God. The devil was a murderer from the very beginning, hence their desire to kill Jesus, doing their father's bidding. "He has nothing to do with the truth, because there is no truth in Him."

In fact "when he lies, he is just speaking out of his own lying nature; he is a liar and the father of lies."

They are not of their father Abraham, nor of Abraham's Father, but of the devil.

Religion would rather believe a lie, than embrace relationship. It seems easier to check off your list of do's and don'ts and leave it at that, than to embrace the light and love of Jesus who has been sent from God, who has spoken only truth as He touched people with His goodness. But all Jesus accusers can say to the Truth is, "Are we not right in saying that you are a Samaritan and have a demon?" [61]

God the Son with a demon…now there is the ultimate contradiction!

Religion has a damnable way of causing those entrapped by it to label the "new move of God" whereby lives are being changed and transformed, people are seeking Jesus more passionately, and signs and wonders are confirming the Word, as the work of the devil.

Since when has the devil's strategy been renewed passion for Jesus?

If this renewal/revival is not of the devil, than judgments are leveled that it is some twisted faith of half-breed Samaritan origin whereby strange fire is being offered up on a different mountain, in another temple administered by charlatan priests. This judgment is made because, "this is not the way God moved before when our faith group was first established by God's outpouring. Now that was genuine revival.

This is the way God moves, not that way!"

So, every new move of God is sadly resisted by the previous move of God, to our shame.

We have sought to "kill" God's current revelation in the earth. We have prayed for awakening, and when God's Spirit came, He did not come the way we envisioned.

So God's spiritual outpouring of true light is deemed darkness. **God help us not to limit what You want to do now by holding to what You have done.**

Jesus knowing they seek to kill Him, zeros in on their death plot against Him. First he denies being possessed or oppressed by a demon. He simply is doing and saying what truly honors the Father while they dishonor Him. His Father is seeking His glory, not He Himself. His Father will judge between them.

Jesus is simply telling them the truth that He has "seen" while with the Father, (8:38)

Here He first discreetly reveals His co-eternal existence with God the Father. So now he expands that thought even further.

"Truly, truly, I say unto you, if anyone keeps My **Word, he will never see death."** [62]

Who is He to be promising eternal life as a result of belief in His Person? Who indeed!

Now He has baited them for the shocking climax of this testy discourse. He is about to turn up the full brilliance of His light. Now they are **convinced** He has a demon.

"Even Abraham died. Yet you say if we keep your word, we will never taste death."

"Are you greater than our father Abraham and the prophets who died? Who do you claim to be?" Jesus responds by again emphasizing that He is speaking the truth as revealed by His Father, their God also. Even the one they proudly claim as their spiritual father, Abraham, looked forward to the day Jesus would come on the scene, he saw it by faith.

The religious leaders are convinced they have Jesus cold, not knowing the lid of this trap is about to come crashing down, on them.

"You are not even fifty; how can you say you have seen Abraham? How indeed?

"Truly, truly, I say unto you, before Abraham was, "I Am." [63]

They pick up stones to kill him. Their final response to the brilliance of His light was to do what was already in their hearts: kill the Son of God. They were ready to stone Him on the spot with no trial. They got it! He was claiming to be God! He called Himself the very same name God called Himself as he identified His name and nature to Moses, "I Am." Blasphemy!

They were blinded by the light!

This is always the result of religion. It kills true revelation, because the light seems to contradict preconceived beliefs, often the traditions of men. In fact, current revelation may be the prophetic fulfillment of former promises yet unrealized. So they cannot "see" the light even though it's very purpose is to open up a whole new world to the King and Kingdom into which they are being invited to participate and through which they are able to fulfill their destiny, to cooperate with the Light and become the people of God's original design.

The glory departs. "Jesus hid himself and went out of the temple." But he did not hide himself from those who were truth seekers.

In fact, He so identifies with his creation that the Pharisees accuse him of being a drunk and a partier. Earlier John says, "As He spoke thus, many believed in Him." [64] He spoke of His origin, his authority, His mission to be lifted up as the Son of man, saying when that happens, they will know "I am He."

He would enter into absolute darkness.

His sacrifice on the cross becomes the "critical mass" that explodes all mankind's dark efforts to save himself, and **leads captives out of the dark kingdom, into the kingdom of Light.**

He explodes His life-giving light so that "even the darkness is as light for all who will follow **The Light**. By going down to the depths, He is exalted to the heights, King of Kings and Lord of Lords, Light of the world. [65]

So in the very next scene, one who was blind from birth is miraculously healed to demonstrate the works of God. [66]

All hell breaks loose among the religious leaders because Jesus healed this man on the Sabbath! The healed man is attempting to enlighten them. They are still so blinded by their "letter of the law" mentality, that they could not see what this simple blind man could see. This man, Jesus, "must be of God or he could do nothing."

After all who ever heard of a person being healed of birth born blindness?

Because they say, "we see," Jesus says, "you are blind, your guilt remains. "I came for those who know they do not see. We are born into blindness. But the people in darkness have seen a great Light!"

While on vacation at the Oregon Caves we experienced total darkness for a few moments. All flashlights were extinguished deep in the belly of the caves. We could almost touch the darkness it was so thick.

Frankly, it was a relief to see the Ranger's light come on again, and subsequently the rest of the tourists' lights. Unspeakable blessing is Christ's brilliance and beauty.

Having seen the Light, we are changed forever, one way or the other.

Just as Saul was at first blinded by Christ's brilliance on the road to Damascus, we need to encounter the brilliant revelation of Christ's light in our hearts. Saul's physical blindness was temporary until He received that same Light into his heart from a "light bearer," sent by Christ Jesus...Ananias.

Saul the murderer was transformed into the Apostle Paul, the "light bearer" to the Gentiles. He immediately began to tell His story, to share the light with whoever would listen.

The Light of Life transforms us into our destiny in Christ's kingdom. We are called to be light bearers.

I tell you the truth. Receive the Light, embrace the light, and stay in the light.

All who acknowledge they are blind will see the Light and be continually filled, becoming a brilliant lamp, a lighthouse if you will, a "city on a hill."

"Thick darkness will cover the earth, but arise, shine, for your light has come and the glory of the Lord has risen upon you! Nations will come to your light, and kings to the brightness of your rising." [67]

Chapter V

One Way

*"**Truly, truly, I say unto you,** he who does not enter the sheepfold by the door but climbs in by another way is a thief and a robber. Truly, truly, I am the door of the sheep." (John 10:1 & 7)*

Jesus begins this discourse by use of a parable in which He states that He is the Door by which one enters into the blessedness of His sheepfold. Anyone entering any other way by any other method such as jumping over the walls, is up to no good.

First thing in the morning, shepherds must enter by the one door, acknowledged by the gatekeeper to tend the sheep.

Anyone coming before Him is a thief and robber coming by stealth of night. As the shepherd leads His sheep out, they follow Him because they know His voice. He walks before them, he does not drive them.

They will not follow a pretender who tries to lead them out. They do not recognize or know any other.

Through His care they are provided with all they need to be abundantly blessed.

While a door or gateway can be both exciting and fearful by reason of not knowing what is on the other side, Jesus being the exclusive entryway into His sheepfold is both intriguing and inviting. Inviting, because in John's brief account to this point we have seen Him to be healer, supplier/provider: inclusive rather than exclusive (Samaritan well); forgiving and gracious to the woman caught in adultery, fearless as He confronts religious bigotry and murderous hatred; and now He invites us to enter His flock through Him.

Jesus was and is still intriguing in His unique bold claims that seekers come to Him for eternal life and abundant life now.

While He is inclusive, inviting whosoever will to come and excluding no one; He is not inclusive regarding the way to Father God.

He is the door and there is no other. So much for modern day "tolerance" and "whatever works for you" and "what is true for you may not be true for me." He is "the" Truth personified, the Truth lived.

Jesus is like His Father in that way…you know, "no other gods…" The Father declares multiple times in

Isaiah and the prophets, "I alone am He, there is no other."

The first command is to worship the Lord your God and acknowledge no other. He is by His own reckoning a "Jealous God." [68] This is no mere human jealousy driven by insecurity and possessiveness. He is jealous in the sense that He commands no encroachment upon His relationship with His beloved any more than a righteous husband would allow a usurper for his wife's affection and intimacy.

He is jealous out of love for His beloved. He knows any other love would be counterfeit and be unable to protect, nourish and provide everything He provides for His lover, His bride.

Perhaps when compared to a marriage covenant this exclusivity is more understandable. What kind of love would it be that allows another lover for one He has vowed to exclusively love? But this is not an analogy men have created; it is God's own analogy throughout the prophets.

He has betrothed His people to Himself. "I have loved you with an everlasting love." [69]

What need have you for a false lover who only wants to exploit you?

Jesus also reflects that same exclusivity in regard to one's spiritual quest. He has this problem, He thinks He is God, the "I AM" and therefore ought to be exclusively sought.

Why?

He alone is *The* **Good Shepherd**, not **a** good shepherd among many. He alone has given His life in exchange for ours. He lays down His life for His sheep. The Apostle Paul said, "There is one God and one mediator between God and man, the man Christ Jesus." [70]

The early church proclaimed the same exclusivity; "Neither is there salvation in any other, for there is no other name under heaven which can save us." [71]

Let's move from the poetic analogy of marital relations, and just think logically: the exclusivity of the Godhead's perspective really does make sense. After all, not all claims to divinity can be true. Only one can be true by even a layman's definition of "God."

The concept of God inherently implies exclusive essence and character. No one else even comes close.

I may worship the sun or moon, a constellation, a teacher, a prophet, or and idea of universal oneness if I wish; but Buddha, nor Allah, nor the "plethora" of gods (small "g") have taken my moral depravity upon themselves and bought my eternal fellowship with the One true God and Father of us all by dying for me.

None has, three days later, risen to life victorious over death. Not one has been seen by numerous witnesses thereafter and at one point, by more than five hundred people.

It is neither logical nor part of human experience for that many people to be delusional, have the same delusion, and die defending that delusion! **He is the way, the door** as He said **the truth and the life.**

Through Him alone is access to the Father Who scripture says had sent Him for this very reason.

Simply try praying to these false "doors" and see if they even acknowledge your existence.

You may not have a statue in your "altar "or place of worship, but the truth about idols aptly applies to these visible or invisible false gods. They have no eyes, ears, hands nor heart that breaks for your loneliness or pain.

They are created by man's own making. They are not the God of Creation. They cannot help you.

For The **Good** Shepherd (His own characterization), I can live, and could by His grace even die, as countless martyrs have for His sake believing that He alone is Lord.

Again, Jesus is not *a* good shepherd among many; He is "The" Good Shepherd who lays down His life for His sheep. A hireling only cares for the money he makes tending the sheep. He would be a rarity who would forfeit His life for them. After all, they are not His.

He has not named them each and developed a special call for each one as He cares for them. A thief only wants the money he could make from slaughtering them for market or selling them to an unscrupulous farmer. But the Good Shepherd willingly gives His life for them… and more.

The classic description of Psalms 23 warmly portrays the guiding, providing, protective, and nurturing care of the Good Shepherd. David bears witness that the Lord as our Shepherd leads us into green pastures, still waters, and restoration.

As He cares for us we are followed by "goodness and mercy all of the days of our lives." [72]

The classic book on Psalm 23, written by a shepherd, points out that in truth, the shepherds in Palestine do not drive their sheep as did some cultures; rather they lead them and call them by name. The sheep can choose to follow or not. They do so because of the covering and provision of one with whom they have relationship. A stranger they will not follow. They know their shepherd's voice and respond to him alone. He has been the one leading them by still waters so they can drink, into lush pasture so they are well fed and all the while protecting them from predators (the wolf) with his rod and staff, no small protection. Many years of practice had sharpened their use of these simple but effective weapons. By these weapons and by His passion for His flock, He protects them from the thief whose purpose is to steal, kill and destroy.

This is of course a classic description of the devil, enemy of our soul. [73]

Even those sheep that are stubborn, lost, or in trouble by reason of their own willfulness, the Good Shepherd will seek out, defend and save from certain destruction. "All we like sheep have gone astray." But He does not beat us into submission. If there is any coercion involved, it is the coercion of love conquering our hearts, desiring to restore us to His flock where He can impart the fullness of His goodness. He carries those pregnant with lambs in His arms as Isaiah depicts.

He picks up and restores those who are "cast" down, (having lain on their side not realizing that this small indent in the terrain is deep enough that they will not be able to get up, they are "cast." They run the risk of respiratory failure or worse, being easy prey for the predators). He uses a preventative balm on their snouts to keep a certain fly from laying larva which will when mature, cause them great harm. He keeps them free of harmful ticks, and doctors them when they are injured.

In Johns' gospel, the Good Shepherd is about to lay down His life for His sheep.

For us, His sheep, He has already laid down His life like a Lamb led to the slaughter who said not a word, except, "Father, forgive them; they know not what they do."

Here Jesus declares that He willingly lays down His life for His sheep. Here He uses the first person; "I" lay down My life. He has the authority to lay it down and to take it up; authority given to Him by His Father Who loves Him.

Love's overflow baptizes, rescues, delivers and heals us. In the counsels of Heaven, before time began God the Son declares, "Lo, I delight to do Your will, a body You have prepared for me."[74] Jesus is not like the hireling who runs from danger.

He runs into it willingly laying down His life to "save" His sheep. His death for His sheep is no accident as it would be for a hired hand.

It is His will and His Father's will. He is in total alignment with that will completely for the sake of His sheep. There is no other way they can be saved from destruction.

The image of the Good Shepherd is perhaps our most enduring image. Children with caring teachers in Sunday school have pictures of the Shepherd in His pastoral setting holding the lambs in His arms. Jesus says on one occasion, "let the little ones come to me, do not hinder them."[75]

Yet sadly, as life happens, and as we are buffeted by its stormy weather, we begin to doubt our Shepherd's goodness. Some of the most awful things are attributed to Him and His Father. Revisiting the

Gospels frequently is the best antidote for the poison of accusation and blame which can permeate our souls when we cannot see past the pain of our immediate crisis.

What Jesus did, He still does.

He carries us in His arms so naturally we often are unaware that we are being carried.

Even when we do not understand after praying so fervently why we or a loved one are not healed, He is still good. Even when life's circumstances and the enemy of our souls would impugn His character and nature, be encouraged He can handle your doubts and even your anger.

However, please choose not to live there.

If you come to the Good Shepherd, His Spirit "The Comforter" comforts as no one else can.

The "why" answer may never come, but the One who is "there" will never forsake or leave you. He is always in you and with you.

Friends and family just gathered to memorialize a father; husband and friend who we felt went to be with Jesus "prematurely" at fifty three. Probably a few thousand people following his progress on "Care Pages" prayed, believed, and hoped for His healing. Though he outlived the doctor's projections, His wife and children and grandchildren no longer can have the intimacy of His presence.

Our comfort is that the Good Shepherd now holds Him mercifully in His loving arms.

As our friend would say, "It doesn't get any better than this." Yet family and friends who believe in God's healing power are in wonderment. "All things work out for good for those who love the Lord," while absolutely true, is an untimely truth right now as we long for a loved one. Only drawing near to the Good Shepherd will be the sustaining power that carries us through the valley of the shadow. It is encouraging to know that the pioneer and "perfector" of our faith has been there before us, knows the way and will be our guide. He is still good even when we do not understand.

The religious leaders of Jesus' day shock us by not only rejecting Him as Good Shepherd, but by as they did in chapter nine, assigning to Him demonic possession and or "madness."

As C.S. Lewis said, there are really only three options in light of the claims Jesus made about himself. One, He is mad, thinking He is co-equal with God. Two, He is a conniving power-hungry liar, knowing all along He is not God's Son and seeking to deceive, making him equal to the devil of hell. Or three, He is Who He says He is: God the very Son.

The religious leaders chose both option one and two which many of that day considered as one.

Isn't it interesting that the word "demon" in John's gospel is only used when Jesus is being accused of being possessed by one or when he is defending himself from being one?

Those who take this tact cannot be bothered with the fact that He healed the blind man. He is simply dismissed.

A friend of mine was attending a lecture given at Portland State by a Muslim who declared that Jesus never said He was equal with God.

My friend boldly said He did, in fact, do so.

The man was so agitated, that he came down the aisle to my friend and railed against him saying He absolutely did not. My friend being a novice believer at the time had not the experience to quote from John's gospel, though he knew this lecturer was wrong.

Why was this man so agitated and angry? Because if Christ is one with God as He so claimed, He would then have to be heard as God, and not a prophet or good man or teacher whose words could be admired, but not be taken seriously as eternal truth.

Allah and the God of Abraham are not in fact the same as some would claim.

Only God the Father, Son and Spirit have always existed and exhibited their Oneness with Trinitarian love, coming as a man, bearing our own burdens, dying sacrificially, raising again, freeing us from sin and offering salvation not by works, but as a gift.

In the next paragraph Jesus alienates the Jewish leaders even more. This scene may have taken place at a later time; nevertheless, He uses the same analogy of Shepherd and sheep to plainly state that He is the Messiah.

He says first, that He has clearly told them already by His life and by the miracles He has done, that He is Messiah. But because they are not His sheep, they cannot receive or believe this revelation. His sheep hear His voice and are known by Him.

They follow Him and He gives them eternal life. In addition, Jesus issues two more great promises; One, they shall never perish: and two, no one will be able to snatch them out of His hand.

Why?

It is because He is greater than all. These two promises are available concurrently with the first two: "We hear His voice," He gives eternal life."Just so they really get the point, He declares again, "I and the Father are one." [76]

His answer was far more than they expected. They are ready to kill Him again by stoning, but first He asks them for which of His good works do they wish to stone Him?

Their answer is none of the above, but, "You make yourself equal with God."[77] Yes, exactly so! But to them, this is blasphemy.

"The Father is in Me and I am in the Father."[78] He is, in fact, not making Himself to be anything. He is both sent by the Father, and endorsed by the Father's testimony.

He simply is what He is. Just as God said to Moses, "I Am that I Am" He further compels them to look at the testimony of His good works which, in fact, are the works of the Father to whom he is subservient during His earthly mission.

He has told them not to believe if "I do not do the works of the Father."[79] But if they study His works, they will "come to know and keep on knowing" just as the blind man had previously stated, that, "these works could not be done by a mere man."

Now they seek to arrest Him when they should have been *arrested* by Him, (stopped in their tracks, so to speak). They should have been captivated by His word of truth that He is the "Door," the "Good Shepherd," and one with the Father. But it was not yet His time, so He escaped from them, though we do not know how.

Even worse, at this final rejection of His true identity, Jesus withdraws from them. He goes back to where John had ministered at the Jordan. Many now come to Him and many believe.

The question remains for anyone exposed to Christ and His claims; "Who do you say I am?" Will you enter through the door and yield your life to the Good Shepherd?

The truth is, He is all that and so much more!

VI

Dying to Live

*"**I tell you the truth,** unless a grain of wheat falls to the ground and dies, it remains only a single seed…. But I when I am lifted up will draw all men unto me, (John 12:24-32).*

The context here is after the triumphal entry when some Greek seekers come saying, "Sir we would see Jesus."[80] The disciples report this to Jesus. His answer was: "Now is the time for the Son of Man to be glorified, so, unless a grain of wheat falls to the ground and dies."[81] "What shall I say, Father, save me from this hour? No, it was for this very reason I came to this hour. Father, glorify Your name."[82] "I have already and will again," answered Father God.[83]

"This voice was for your benefit, not mine," Jesus clarified. "It is time for judgment on this world.

The prince of this world will be driven out.

But I, when I am lifted up from the earth, will draw all men unto me." [84]

As he draws within a couple of days of His death at Calvary, the overall theme is the glorification of Christ by His Father. I find it fascinating that this is the response of Jesus to the entreaty of the Greeks who asked His disciples, "Sir, we would see Jesus." It is as if He is saying, "If you would see Jesus clearly, see Him in the fullness of His mission as 'Son of Man' to glorify the Father and to be glorified by His Father. See Him in the context of His Isaac-like subservience to His Father (which has direct implications regarding how we treat each other in Christ's family).

See Him lifted up, suspended between heaven and earth "becoming sin who knew no sin." See Him in context of laying down His life as a kernel of wheat, for whoever will believe.

The end result, rather than losing life, will be gaining eternal life as His follower.

Later Saint Paul will pray that he might know Christ in His suffering, in His sacrificial giving of His life. We are taught to embrace the cross-life by the example of Jesus and His early followers. We have died with Him and now are held in the cleft of the Rock who is Jesus, and we arise to new life.

Father will honor one who serves in such abandonment. [85]

The further consequence of Christ's willingness to die as that grain of wheat is that he can reproduce many seeds.

See Him as the "Seed" of Abraham by which God promised to multiply innumerable seeds all endued with a God-given capacity to reproduce. Through Christ the Abrahamic blessings of the God of Israel are now realized in everyone who will believe and receive "the promise of the Spirit."[86] "God is the Father of us all who gives life to the dead and calls things that are not as though they were."

The wonder of the Father heart of God is that he wants the Triune fellowship to be broad, to invite and embrace a huge family. He has revealed that truth from the very beginning of recorded Biblical history.

Jesus is the first fruits of abundant fruit, followers who having died with Christ, are raised up into many grains of wheat, much fruitfulness, ultimately bread to feed the nations. Think of the fluffy white head of the dandelion upon which you blew and the seeds floated away empowered by your breath.

So it is with the seed which comes from Christ's burial in the tomb; much grain is being spread, planted and reproduced, empowered by the wind of the Spirit.

Further He is saying, "See me" in the context of judgment being rendered to this world and its evil prince being driven out. Jesus Himself, as He is lifted up on the cruel cross, will draw all men unto Him while annulling the authority of the prince of evil.

This is further explained by the Apostles. The devil is still present, not cast out from the earth. But according to Paul in his letter to Ephesus, the enemy only has authority through those who are rebellious to Jesus the One Who has won authority over all things.

Christ now holds the keys of death and Hades, taken from the vile serpent by His humble death at Calvary. In His willingness to provide a body, to become the Lamb of God, standing in for the Pascal Lamb of Passover, He once and for all provided the sacrifice that absorbed and appeased the wrath of God (a wrath which is a natural consequence of His holiness wherein sin must be paid for).

In so doing He fulfills perfectly the law of God on our behalf so that now we are declared the righteousness of God in Christ! He is as Paul says the "Just and the Justifier."[87] His judgment, "the wages of sin is death, but the free gift of God is eternal life!"

"We are saved by grace through faith."[88] Our old man, or sin nature is dead in the waters of baptism.

To "see" Jesus, we must understand Him as "lifted up," the description He used to declare what kind of death He would die. [89]

We must understand that to a Jew, and to a Roman, the cross was shameful. Romans administered capital punishment to their citizens by beheading.

So, Paul was reported to have been beheaded. The cross was saved only for murders and political insurgents, perhaps disloyal slaves. The Jews viewed hanging on the cross as a curse.[90] So anyone who hung on a tree was under God's curse.

The Apostle Paul capitalized on this viewpoint by saying Jesus became accursed for us so that we could be delivered from the curse of the law.[91] The shamefulness and indignity endured by the Son was unthinkable. God, the very God being abused, spat upon, toyed with during multiple horrible beatings and mocking.

What marvelous love for us was manifested in His restraint!

Paul states that Satan, had He understood the outcome, would not have crucified Jesus. But he seemed to understand that Jesus was not going to defend Himself.

Satan did some of his most grotesque work through both Roman guards and Jewish leaders, punishing Jesus to the utmost.

Yet it all played right in to the redeeming plan of the Godhead. For it was by His stripes that we have been healed, He took our offenses our punishments, our psychological pain, our iniquities, our infirmities, our disease, and for the first time seemingly, abandonment from the Father.[92]

As Phil Yancy says so eloquently, "No theologian can adequately explain what happened within the Trinity on that day at Calvary. All we have is the cry of a child who felt forsaken."[93]

Not only that, but there was for Jesus, no "last minute" deliverance from the suffering of death which Abraham and Isaac had experienced at the altar. Rather than a ram in the bush, Jesus himself was the sacrifice that the Father was now providing for us all, once and for all, so we now can come boldly before the throne of God and find grace and mercy in time of need.[94]

As a consequence, in that awful death, what looked like ultimate defeat for Jesus, actually was a deathblow for Satan who was publically defeated and whose head was crushed as God had promised in the Genesis account of man's fall from grace. Furthermore, the accusations that stood against us were annulled and nailed to the cross.[95]

Finally Jesus is saying, "See Me as the light."

He repeats this theme having made much of it earlier in John's account of the gospel, in answer to the religious leaders asking, "Who is this 'Son of Man' who will die by being lifted up?" (My paraphrase). They seem to understand He was speaking of dying since they said scripture teaches that this Messianic figure will live forever.

They clearly linked this "Son of Man" saying with the prophecies regarding the Messiah.

"Son of Man" is Jesus' favorite expression of His person and it usually includes His prophetic destiny. The name is diminutive like John's "the disciple whom Jesus loves."

At the very least, it is an expression that embraces our human condition compassionately.

He became one of us.

Scholars argue whether or not it is a title synonymous with Messiah, or just a poetic expression, as in Daniel for "a human being."

These leaders seem to have understood it as the former. So Jesus' answer is that they should respond to Messiah, Son of Man, walking in His light before the darkness overtakes them. They must put their trust in the light so they can be "sons of light."

 Further on He states that He has come into the world as light so no one has to stay in the darkness... if they believe.[96] Truth flows from this "Light" bearing us out of the kingdom of darkness and into the Kingdom of Light?

The truth is that the way up is down in God's workings. A kernel of wheat must die in humility to be reborn.

Christ came, laying aside His glory and His co-equality for a season, becoming a Servant Who said," I came to serve, not to be served."

He understood that there could be no crown without the cross though He was tempted by the devil to take shortcuts. He was cloaked in humility. "He came to His own but His own did not receive Him."[97] He exercised authority by washing His disciples' feet, a job reserved for the lowest non-Jewish slave.

He exercised power by laying down His life willingly so that we could live. He would not save Himself, instead, He chose to save us.

Author Phil Yancy asks his usual penetrating question: Do we look at Jesus' powerlessness as an example of God's impotence, or as proof of God's love? His death on the cross in the Jewish mindset was proof against His being Messiah. His crucifixion was a fulfillment of the curse of the law for anyone hung on a tree.

The Romans saw nothing God-like in another "religio-political" upstart claiming kingship.

But, as Yancy points out, Jesus did not affirm His kingship until it was too late to be taken seriously. Karl Barth said, "He does not confess His Messiahship until the moment when the danger of founding a religion was past."

Knowing the cross was preordained, decided in the counsels of heaven, foretold by poet and prophet, is an unmistakable illustration of God's love for us through His Son. He says at one point, "I confer upon you a kingdom."

His invitation is to take up our cross and follow Him. Not exactly Madison Avenue in its appeal.

What can He mean by conferring upon us a kingdom?

Isn't that later, after the second coming?

No, He breathes on His apostles His Holy Spirit and then weeks later at Pentecost He pours out His Spirit which supernaturally gifts His followers with power from on high: Power to be His witnesses in Jerusalem, Judea, Samaria, and the outermost parts of the world. The cross and our belief in the One who gave His life there, was the means by which we could become members of His Kingdom.

Kingdom Building

It was the gospel of His Kingdom which He preached. Salvation is the means by which we enter into His Kingdom. **That is important**.

One might think having studied today's churches that salvation is their ultimate mission (though in America, we are not doing well, even with that calling). But

Jesus had a higher purpose. He is building a kingdom through which nations within nations, without borders, bow to Him only in fulfilling His commission to transform the earth.

He even taught His followers to pray, "Your kingdom come, Your will be done on earth as it is in heaven." **Our primary mission is to be vessels through which He works His transformation and restoration**.

We are kingdom builders, but not our own kingdoms, His kingdom.

What does His kingdom in heaven look like?

There is complete wholeness and restoration.

So it should also be on the earth. Our prayers should call down heaven to earth, creating an atmosphere where Christ the King can rule and reign. He is enthroned upon the praises of His people.[98]

As we call upon Him in worship and prayer and honor him with obedient lives, it creates a landing strip for Him to come and be enthroned so He can rule and reign as King in our circumstances, and initiate His rulership in the earth.

Not only are we servants, but friends to whom he reveals what He is about to do.

Through this new prophetic community also called the church, the assembly, the called out ones, He will make known the mystery of His will to principalities and powers.

All authority is given Him in heaven and earth, He now confers that authority to His followers, those kernels of wheat willing to go into the ground, having died to their old nature now embracing their new nature as saints of the most High. No longer paupers, but kings and priests.[99]

Just as there was a cross before the crown for Jesus, so it also is for us. Paul prays to know Him even in His suffering. And so we say with the disciple, Thomas, on the way to see Jesus raise Lazarus, "let us go so we may die also," and be raised to new life.[100]

What is it in our lives that the Holy Spirit may be fingering, a thing which hinders our stepping into the fullness of our destiny in His kingdom?

Let us see ourselves as a grain of wheat, planted in the soil of Christ's word, ready to die so we may live and produce much fruit in our dying.

Let us love our life by losing it for His Kingdom's sake, for Christ's sake.

Let us follow Him and become like He is in every quality and character of His person, filled with all His fullness, a kingdom of priests.

A Servant is Not Greater than His Master

John13

"Truly, truly I say unto you a servant is not greater than his master, nor is he who is sent greater than he who sent him," (13:16).

Truly, truly I say unto you, he who receives any one whom I send receives Me; He who receives Me receives Him Who sent Me." (20)

"Truly, truly I say to You, one of you will betray Me." (21)

This passage begins with the Lord humbly washing His disciple's feet. The shock factor of Jesus' behavior as He condescends to wash his disciple's feet is lost to our era. It would be something like a famous surgeon wiping bottoms in a retirement home, or like a president serving us at a restaurant.

The custom of foot-washing was a necessity not a ritual or nicety, if you had the time to do it. Feet and sandals carried barnyard odors like Joseph and Mary would have smelled at Jesus' birth, like animal feces, smell of urine at times, dust, grime and sweat.

Walking the roads in this era was a dirty experience for everyone's feet. No one had offered do this lowly job of foot-washing.

The lowest man on the servant pecking order was chosen because it was such a disgusting task. Jesus smelled of the smells of humanity just like us. He had become one of us.

But unlike us, He turned the foulness of our condition into the beautiful fragrance of His servant's heart, for He was born into the foulness of our condition. He was touched by it just as we are, and now He enters into His passion with a prophetic act illustrating His spirit of humble sacrifice, "servanthood," and the ultimate purification enacted for us at Calvary.

So here they were, sitting at the table with the King of Kings and Lord of Lords, who was unafraid to get soiled with our daily lives.

Instead he provided the only remedy.

This night was the beginning of His passion, "showing them the full extent of how much he loved them."[101]

John states the astounding truth that Jesus knew all power was given to Him by His Father who had sent Him and to whom He was about to return.

How does He illustrate this power? He humiliates Himself by performing the lowliest of acts of service. Master displays His power with a bowl and towel, not a crown and scepter. Astounding!

The crown will come later. The return of the King will be with glorious splendor, with not one but many crowns, striking fear into many, but great joy in those longing for His return.

He will come as King of Kings and Lord of Lords on a white horse, regal in splendor awful and terrible in demeanor, His name is Faithful and True.

But for now, only a towel and bowl will do. His disciples must be shown; first of all, His unfathomable love exemplified in washing their feet, and in so doing, be shown how His appointed leaders exercise leadership in His kingdom.

They are also the ones with the towel and bowl. Look for them in the lowliest places, if indeed you may find them.

So He begins His extravagant and surprising illustration. He authentically poured out His love in this act. But He is also teaching, ever teaching, as He inhabits this earth-suit we all wear. He is saying, "*This* is how you love one another; *this* is how you lead." First shall be last and last shall be first.

But Peter is incensed and declares as it were that He will be "damned" if Jesus is going to wash his feet. And Jesus agrees. Jesus' whole life and ministry agrees with Peter.

All of us, not just Peter, would have been lost in damnation if not for the Master's cleansing and purifying ministry.

The foot washing seems to be a symbolic act for what has already happened. Having given their lives to follow Him, they are cleansed as they walk with the King. As He has shown over and over by His life and ministry, instead of our grime making Him dirty, He transforms and purifies us. We stand before Father God by reason of Jesus' sacrificial offerings both here in the upper room, and on the tree of crucifixion where He takes all the filth of the world and the world's spirit and buries it with Him.

Now we are clean and cleansed continually.

Oh Happy day!

He pronounces us eternally clean, and adds that daily purification needed for His followers to wash away the dust, grime, and smell of wrestling with the enemy and interacting with those lost who need Messiah so desperately.

So when Jesus says, if Peter will not allow Him to wash his feet he can have no part of Him, Peter, being who he is, says, "Then wash all of me."

Jesus says no, there is no need for that, just your feet so the dust and filth of the world at this point in time will be washed away. It is as if He were saying, "You know Peter, you are already clean by your association with Me, the Refiner's Fire. You just need what all my followers need, daily washing by the water of the Spirit and the Word." I Am, the Word and Spirit wash you now.

Peter will soon need this daily cleansing as He will shortly deny His association with His Lord.

Peter's Denial

Living on this side of the cross, we know that the outcome of Peter's largest failure, denial of the Lord, was full restoration.

He was willing to humble himself before the Lord as Jesus asked him three times, "Peter, do you love me?"[102] He was willing to become the servant to Christ's body that Jesus here illustrates. Even in the light of Peter's failure to stand with Him during His loneliest night of intercession in the garden and in his death, even in Peter's public denial, He knows Peter loves him.

So He affirms him and challenges him to be a shepherd like **The** Shepherd, laying down his life for the sheep. Peter passionately took this exhortation to heart as history has him in Rome in His last days where he refused to be hung on a cross except upside down.

He thought himself unworthy of dying in the same position as His Savior, the Servant of all!

I find great solace in this story of restoration recorded only John's gospel. Jesus herein shows us that even in light of our own denial of Him, our failure to live in such a way that we illustrate His compassion and mercy rather than judgment; that He knows our true heart, and our true destiny. He declares His love unconditionally again over us, and speaks His destiny into us saying, "Feed my sheep."[103]

Feed the lost wanderers, the walking dead for whom He gave His life.

Feed the ones he wept over as He came into Jerusalem. The servant is not greater that his Master.

Master carries the young ones in His arms, the ones who are with child in process of birthing new levels of their destiny. He will lead His flock like a Shepherd, Isaiah declares.

Jesus illustrates the Father's heart for us.

So what will you do with a God who washes your feet?

Betrayal

In contrast, Judas, rejects the mercy of the Lord which triumphs over judgment. Scripture says He was already infected by the evil one.

Evidently Jesus would not embrace Judas' definition of a Messiah. This Messiah will not be controlled by anything or anyone trying to force his own agenda on Him and His God-ordained mission. He listens only to the voice of His Father. He will not be controlled by the righteous Pharisees, the traditional Priests, the

Zealots, or the revolutionaries who would attempt to overthrow the occupying empire of Rome.

He is not tamable or trainable; He is totally unpredictable and irreligious. Therefore, He must be killed.

Religion must kill what it cannot control.

This Messiah was out of control. Loving the unlovable, touching the diseased and contagious, and forgiving the adulterous, reaching out to the Samaritans, healing on the Sabbath. He has power, all power bequeathed by God the Father.[104] but He will not use that power to take shortcuts to His kingship. No, as many devotional writers have taught us, first the cross, then the crown, not the other way around, not for the Son of Man.

Even this favorite name for Himself, "Son of Man," illustrates Jesus' humility. He has totally embraced humankind with all its frailties and pain, with all its wilderness wanderings looking for love in all the wrong places, with its idolatrous spirit wanting to serve a god it can see, rather than serve the unseen Lover of its Soul.

This Son of Man has wept with Mary and Martha, rejoiced with Lazarus, the prototype of His own death, burial and resurrection.

He wept over Jerusalem desiring to gather them as a mother hen does her chicks; but they would not be gathered into the bosom of the very one they prayed for longingly each Sabbath and Passover.

He would ache for Peter in intercession as Satan desired to test Peter. Before His passion, after this meal, His heart is set upon His destiny at Calvary, He takes great pains, three chapters as John recollects, comforting and preparing His disciples. He is perfect God, perfect man.

The pop song asks, "What if God were one of us?"

He **is** one of us, God with skin, Emanuel, God with us.

 "**I tell you the truth;** one of you is going to betray me." Judas sadly had his own agenda, and Jesus would not go there. So he betrays the Son of Man.

But Judas was not alone, Jesus confronts Peter's boasting declaration that he would follow Jesus to hell and back and says, "**I tell you the truth,** before the rooster crows, you will deny me three times."[105] In point of fact, all of the disciples denied Him except for John and Jesus' mother along with other significant women who supported Jesus' ministry.

In Peter we see our own failures to stand up for Jesus. In our western culture, asserting our faith might elicit various forms of persecution. Often we think that means to declare what we as believers are against.

Our nation is sick and tired of hearing that.

We are to demonstrate His real character, to **be** Him to broken people, to demonstrate that mercy triumphs over judgment, to invite his miracle working power to the one sitting next to us at our office who has a painful back. We are to go the extra mile in giving of our resources and selves to those who could never pay us back.

So often I have misrepresented the beauty and grace of our Savior, not by actions, but by inactions. He wants us to love his lost sheep the way he loves them.

Forgive us, Lord, when we misrepresent You, or fail to represent You at all.

He declares that He has washed the disciples' feet in love as an example of how they are to treat one another.

Why?

"**I tell you the truth**, no servant is greater than his master or messenger greater than the one who sent Him."[106] He has placed Himself in submission to the Father while on this earth mission even though He is co-equal with the Father, co-eternal, and co-existent.

He is God incarnate, one with the Father.

But while He is here, He does and says only what He sees the Father saying and doing.

"No servant is greater than His Master."

Why is this comparison so important?

It is because we are sent even as He was sent. We are subservient to the Father even as Jesus was. It means that we embrace our God-ordained destiny even as Jesus did, setting his face like flint as he went into Jerusalem, knowing full well it meant His painful death. Sounds pretty scary, like an adventure we would rather forego, like Frodo Baggins in *Lord of the Rings,* a courier who fears that the consequences of delivering the contents of His parcel may result in his own death. And in reality, it may. Hundreds of thousands each year around the world give their lives for the gospel.

However, even if we are not called to martyrdom, then let us say like Thomas, having been told with the disciples that Lazarus is dead, "Let us also go that we may die with Him" (Lazarus).[107]

There is a dying we all must embrace, the dying accomplished at Calvary on our behalf so we are no longer enslaved to sin.

But also we must die to **our** own ambitions and visions, dying to **our** descriptions of **our** destiny, and embrace the Father's destiny for us. If in leadership, we must die to the magnetic appeal to take shortcuts and adopt Madison Avenue methods, die to the motivating of our congregations by guilt.

We must die to the pressure to try and be so much like our culture, rather than a prophetic voice to our culture. If we succumb to cultural pressure we become nothing to anyone, irrelevant, having lost our prophetic voice.

"No servant is greater than his Master."

Just as Jesus was tempered in the fires of affliction, if we are living for Him, so we will be. It is a prerequisite for His disciples, all of whom will be leaders at some level. But here is the promise that keeps us even in the fires of affliction. "**I tell you the truth**, whoever accepts anyone I send accepts Me; and whoever accepts Me, accepts the One who sent Me."[108] We are vessels of honor, Paul later would say; carriers, conduits, ambassadors, and declarers of very good news, by our lives, filled with the person and character of the Only wise God.

We preach by our lives and as a great father of faith has said, "If necessary, use words." We come not to argue with the philosophers (even Saint Paul could not win them over in Athens), but we come with the simple but profound good news." And this good news' name is Jesus. It is He that Paul and the Apostles proclaim, not with words of lofty wisdom, but with the simplicity of the gospel, and with the signs and wonders that confirm the gospel.

Jesus promised to those who would speak forth His message in faith that it would do what He said: convince, convict and convert without condemning or coercing, and frankly, without promises of any "easy street" on this earth.

Who is the One Who has sent us? This is the One, the One Who said not a word in His own defense as He stood before authorities, the One who would have most assuredly received Judas into his merciful arms even after Judas' betrayal. Does He not do so now, even in the face of our many betrayals?

This is the Good Shepherd who never hurt but always healed any who came to him.

The One who is touched with our infirmities, Who now walks in the heavenly throne room with the scars of our redemption still on His hands, head and side, the very Desire of the Nations, the lover of our souls, the giver of good news, binder of broken hearts, liberator of the oppressed, declarer of the year of Jubilee where all was forgiven (compared to one day of judgment in the final days of our earth dwelling), and in which all of us get a "do-over," over and over and over again.

This is He who loved Judas unconditionally knowing full well that he would betray Him.

This is He Who still loves us, knowing we also will at times betray Him and His kingdom purposes when the heat is on, our livelihood is at stake, or we want to be accepted by our peers.

How pitiful an exchange, thirty pieces of Silver, inconceivably incomparable with all He offers us as His servants. How pitiful also the lack of eternal substance for which I betray Him, to which I turn for comfort, rather than turning to the "God of all Comfort."

"**I tell you the truth**, one of you is going to betray me."[109] Here is Jesus' warning to give Judas an alternative direction. But still Judas betrays Him! And so do we at times.

But mercy and grace were and still are available. Tragedy of tragedies, instead of running to Jesus (as Peter did upon seeing Him on the beach after His resurrection) to receive grace and mercy; Judas destroys himself. How little he seems to have learned of the character of Jesus! How he would have been forgiven and welcomed back like the Prodigal son by a Father who is crazy about him and a Savior who will shortly died for Him as part of the family He loves.

 The reason it has been stated so often that He would have died just for you and I if we were the only ones on this fallen planet is simply this. In one sense, He did.

He is so unfathomable in His wisdom, so timeless in His perception, so miraculous in the brilliance of His being, that as He dies for His family, and He also dies for me individually.

Simply put, He can give full attention to me, while also doing so to all His family. His mind is so great that even though He sees all time in a linear fashion, alpha and omega, beginning and end, He sees Jesus, in point of time dying for we His family, and for each individual in His family. Simultaneously, He sees all of humanity who He longs to have in His family, those chosen before the foundations of the world. They are chosen not because they chose, they chose because they are chosen. It is a mystery for sure.

Not only that, but the very, very good news is that at the same time the Father sees us denying Him at some level, He sees Christ's blood, shed at Calvary covering my failure and says, "that is not who you are (put your name in the space). He sees my feet made of clay, but in my heart of hearts, the heart He gives is a heart like William Wallace of *Brave Heart* fighting the evil one; a heart like Frodo overcoming every resistance with the help of his devoted partner Sam in *Lord of the Rings*.

Sam in the epic story can be compared to the Holy Spirit in our lives.

Sam could not and must not carry the ring of power. It was not his assignment. But like the Holy Spirit, Sam carried the ring bearer on His shoulders. And so the Spirit carries us even in our faltering ineptitude, and calls us to a higher destiny than we could ever imagine.

How much we also need each other to fulfill our given destiny.

We have each been given an assignment for the King and the kingdom. He sees us as kings and priests.[110] His calling for us is to be Kingdom makers, not of our own kingdom, but His. The way we accomplish that task is to be like our Master.

"As He is in the world, so are we."

Jesus says through Paul's experience, "My grace is sufficient," and through Saint Peter's, "I know you love me" (my words, implied in the dialogue). Keep on feeding my sheep." "This is your destiny." "I affirm that you and your testimony are the Rock upon which I am building my church."

We are children of destiny, His destiny. We are not disqualified by reason of our failures, rather, in the brokenness of those humiliating experiences we learn how faithful Jesus is, how unaffected and un-surprised He is at our human frailties.

Although He does not minimize sin, He requires neither ritualistic penitence nor groveling. He readily forgives and speaks words of encouragement that retool and recalibrate us towards our aim: piercing the bull's eye of the target of His high-calling.

We are to forget the past keeping our eyes on His face of Mercy.

Chapter VIII

From Grief to Joy

I tell you the truth, you will weep and mourn while the world rejoices you will grieve but your grief will turn to joy. A woman giving birth to a child has pain because her time has come, but when her baby is born, she forgets the anguish because of her joy that a child is born into the world. Now is your time of grief, but I will see you again and rejoice, and no one will take way your joy, (John 16:20-21).

The world is about to rejoice at its most hideous of crime, an unthinkable evil, to torture God.

Of course, more physically painful tortures have come from the mind of evil men, mass ethnic cleansing of unthinkable proportions.

Yes, there have been many guilty persons who have been wrongfully convicted.

But no one has ever, or will ever again torture and murder God the very God; God the Son of Man, manifest holiness and purity, goodness beyond belief. Perhaps we have become dull to the gospel account.

When the Campus Crusade volunteers show the Jesus film in other countries to simple people in simple villages, many who have never heard of Jesus, they weep, they cry out at the injustices and tragedy of Jesus' death; He had only helped, healed and loved unconditionally those to whom He ministered.

But Peter declares in the first post resurrection sermon that this heinous act was to fulfill all righteousness. Righteousness was fulfilled by the One who was perfect God and Perfect man. So it had to be.

The evil one played right in to God's, "deeper magic, "as C.S. Lewis calls it in the *Lion, Witch and Wardrobe.* Saint Paul declares later that "the wages of sin is death, but the free gift of God is salvation through Jesus Christ." [111]

Up until now, a substitute scapegoat bore the sins of Hebrew believers away once a year on the Day of Atonement as the Lamb was sacrificed unto the Lord on the altar and His blood sprinkled on the Ark of Covenant.

By this means they could be right with God for another year. But now in the fullness of time, Jesus came as a substitutionary sacrifice once and for all, His blood buying us back from judgment and eternal death because of our sin nature.

God Himself is the only One who could pay this price. Who else could be perfectly holy, without blemish, just as the Lamb each year was to be without blemish. What man could be wholly pure to become a ransom for one person, much less all mankind?

Only the pure and spotless Lamb of God could be acceptable to buy us back or save, and transport us into eternal light and life.

Priceless love, offered without qualifications is what drew people to Him. He only says "believe I Am Who My words and life declare Me to be."

There are no strings, no hidden clauses if you will no other shoe to drop. This is really a free gift unlike many free offers we receive in the mail. There is always a catch, is there not?

Paul spells it out more completely than any other Apostle. We are saved not by what we do but by believing in Jesus as the Christ, and receiving His free gift of redemption.

"Freely you have received, freely give."

But wait! Does He not require that we live as servants to Him? Require? Servants?

How about family and friends? To say He requires would be like saying to one's spouse on ones wedding day, "I love you unconditionally, I'll always love you and never leave you, but you must love me in return. You must serve me."

No, Jesus is not into slavery.

Yes, we can call ourselves His willing servants as the Apostle Paul often does. But Jesus really lived His life and spoke in such a way that we understand that what He desires is a passionate lover, not an indentured servant.

Consider the Prodigal Father for a moment. Henry Nouwen reflects on the Heart of the Father in Jesus' story.

> *It strikes me that the wayward son had rather selfish motivations. He said to himself, "How many of my father's servants have more food than they want, and her I am dying of hunger!*
>
> *I will leave this place and go to my father." No, He didn't return because of renewed love for his*

father. No, he returned simply to survive. He had discovered that the way he had chosen was leading him to death. Returning to his father was a necessary step for staying alive. He realized that he had sinned, but this realization came about because sin had brought him close to death.

I am moved by the fact that the father did not require any higher motivation. His love was so total and unconditional that he simply welcomed his son home.

Nouwen goes on to say how encouraging, that God does not require a higher motivation before receiving us back. Most of our motivations are, in fact, selfish.

We desire peace, He is peace. Our sins did not satisfy us the way we thought they would.

God's love will always take us back.

Recently I was privileged to lead worship at a men's retreat on the Oregon cost. The guest speaker was Jerry Cook whose church, years ago in Gresham had been the incubator of my launching into worship ministry for over thirty years now. He has grown ever wiser and still is one of the best communicators of the good news I have ever heard.

At one point we were asking him questions. We were talking about God's love, acceptance and forgiveness, the title of Pastor Jerry's first book. I tried to wax wise by saying that God's grace and mercy, His unconditional love flows partly from the fact that He already knows what we are going to do in His timeless view of our existence.

Pastor Jerry looked right at me as if no one else was there and said, "He expects nothing of you."

I was dumfounded.

I could not get my mind around what I knew in my head was true. In my heart I still could never do enough.

I am brother number two in the introduction of Chuck Swindle's book, *In the Grip of Grace,* who decides that instead of mingling with the villagers and starting a home rather than waiting for his father to come and find the three of them. Instead of becoming a judge on top of the hill as his older brother had done, keeping count of all his younger brother's transgressions while waiting for father to come, he would get back to father by his own efforts.

He was lost with his brothers and swept away by the river even though father had warned them not to go in too deep. They were told if this were to happen, to wait, their father would come and find them. Their own efforts would get them even more lost.

So, he decides to build a rock pathway in the river since the river brought him here.

There he is picking up one stone at a time instead of waiting for his father to come to him. What a great word picture of religion; working so hard to reach God when He has made it so easy by reaching out to us.

He invites us to, "Only believe."

I have had two breakdowns while in the ministry for thirty years. One happened in 97, when I was the "March for Jesus" coordinator in Portland and for the State of Oregon while also fulfilling my ministry as fulltime worship pastor. I was functioning outside my gifting as an administrator for an event that brought out ten thousand people. I just want to see the city worship Jesus in the streets.

And so we did. But in the three years I facilitated it, I was getting closer and closer to acute burn out. My own churches pastoral responsibilities were more demanding than most churches. In short, I was doing way too much. But if it had not been the March, it would have been something else. I so wanted our city to experience revival.

Anything that would help launch that kind of revival, I wanted to be a part of. But in my heart of hearts, there were issues of insecurity, inordinate need for recognition by my peers, and an attitude of having to earn God's favor. I finally "hit the wall" and experienced debilitating panic attacks and at the same time, severe, dark depression.

It took much grace from my home church, medication and counseling for me to make my way back to a fully functioning person and pastor. I learned a lot about boundaries and learning to take care of myself better.

Eleven years later, another breakdown happened when we agonized as a leadership team over some trust issues that ultimately broke apart fellowship in a church plant and caused a couple we really love to feel betrayed by us. I was so torn up.

I learned that I am not enough. I could not reconcile three couples all of whom I loved.

Even with an arbitrator, reconciliation escaped us. I found myself in "breakdown" mode again because of this issue while also taking care of my mother in law at home for a year. She was in late stages of Alzheimer's.

I simply felt like a failure in every area of my life and battled with panic attacks and depression again. The Lord healed more layers by His visitations and by help from a great counselor and support from a loving fellowship of those who stayed together.

The positive side is that I believe we are growing healthy followers and real relationships in a home church setting now.

Recently I was rear-ended on my way to a church to lead worship. For the next five to six weeks, even though my pain was soft tissue stuff, I was not getting adequate sleep.

The accident aggravated my herniated disk problem that I have dealt with for a decade.

With my history, sleep is absolutely critical.

I was not getting better with physical therapy, and I was taking too much pain medication for my livers' sake. So my nurse practitioner prescribed a prednisone pact. I was to take four pills a day for four days, three for three days, and two for two days tapering off to one. It was like pouring jet fuel down my gullet. I could not sleep at all. I went into a tail spin of manic behavior and ended up in the psych ward for a weekend after getting lost overnight on a mountain trail.

I was making bad judgments due to lack of sleep. By the time I was admitted to the psych ward, I had been walking all night to get out of the mountains but, I was not tired even after being up thirty hours and having walked 10 to 20 miles. My family who had been up all night worrying about me had to convince me for two hours to go in for evaluation.

I was diagnosed as Bi-Polar after that weekend and given a new medication. That just made me worse. I was so badly manic and sleep deprived I ended up hallucinating.

I was admitted again to the psych ward for seven days in which time I was finally given the right combination of meds for Bi-Polar condition. Looking back on my two earlier breakdowns I now can see that the last stages of recovery in both of them was classic manic behavior.

My family witnessed this, my pastoral staff, but not my counselor, I had not presented that way in his office, so, no one knew.

The misdiagnosis of prednisone was to say the least, hellish for me and my family.

After being released from the hospital, once more I had to take baby steps back to normalcy where I could function and actually do well. Three weeks out, I was able to attend a church where not that many people know my pastoral background or my current journey back to health while on Bi-Polar medications. It was a safe place where I could go and no one expected anything of me.

I just bawled as worship began for the first couple of weeks, barely able to take in where I had been and wondering where I was going.

I was grieving over the experience. God's Spirit was hovering over me, loving me and reassuring me that I was going to be alright, even flourish in this season of my life at sixty three. Bi-polar is a foul-up in the receptors of my neurons synapses wherein there may be too much adrenalin at times and too little at other times causing higher highs and lower lows than normal. When compared to challenges and trials others go through, this one is temporary provided I stay on my meds.

It is difficult, albeit, but not, except for God's grace, insurmountable. Regulating stress, proper sleep and diet are essential.

Support from family and friends essential. Dependence on the Lord, of course, is absolute. I will need to continue taking meds the rest of my life unless God heals me.

But God heals in many ways.

My own stream of the body of Christ has been very insensitive towards those who are on anti-depressants, or other "receptor up-take meds." Sometimes what we are dealing with is chemical imbalance in the brain.

God gave us minds so we could develop these kinds of meds to help people. I consider these meds a part of God's grace.

"Weeping may tarry for the night, but joy comes in the morning."

Life happens!

It often humbles us, confuses us, disappoints us, and even shatters our hopes and dreams at times, all things the apostles are about to experience. But Light comes and His name is Jesus. He walked this lonesome valley by himself, but not really by Himself.

His Father was with Him as was the Holy Spirit. There are "hidden treasures in the dark places"[112] that we could never receive anywhere else. I am encouraged that each time we experience darkness, as we cry out to Him, we experience a new level of light, new intimacy with Him. If we hold on to Him, seek his face, we will as the scripture says, "look to Him and our faces will be made radiant."

We are delivered into his radiance through the birthing canal of trials and tribulations. When the new life arrives, joy arrives and sorrow is forgotten.

"Jesus said you will have trouble in this world, but take heart; I have overcome the world."[113]

How?

By the anguish of His passion in which as pioneer of our faith, He took our grief and sorrow, our pain and tribulation, our iniquity and sin, our infirmities and diseases into His own person, and absorbed and transformed them He birthed a brand new kingdom with a brand new kind of man and woman, a restored man and woman, after the original design of Eden.

No more separation, no more hiding from Him. It is unnecessary.

Yes, we at times are guilty of individual sins. But we are not guilty, because he forgives His repentant children. Both truths stand in amazing juxtaposition.

He demands nothing but desires passionately our love. He wants to be wanted. He hides at times, to be found by us.

Astonishingly, He makes Himself vulnerable so that He longs for and even expresses need for our love as a husband does His wife's love.

He submits this beautiful word picture to us, not the reverse! He invites us to experience infinite pleasure at His right hand, an obvious reference to sexuality between husband and wife, meant to be applied to soul to soul intimacy, spirit to spirit, deep calling unto deep as David says.[114]

He calls Israel His bride. His heart is broken when they adulterate themselves with idols.

He laments loudly as they turn to other lovers throughout the prophets. Somehow, wonder of wonders, we complete Trinitarian love and fellowship!

When we come to Him and confess our faults and failures, He says to us, "go and sin no more." He does not say, "Here are your steps of penance."

But what if we do fail again?

He separates our sin from us as far as the east is from the west the Psalmist says.[115] If you started going east right now how far would you have to go to finally be going west? It will never happen!

That is why David uses such language.

He loses our sin in the sea of forgetfulness. So when we say "again" there is no "again."

As we confess to Him, it is the same as never having done this before. Does that mean we should not seek help for besetting sin or addiction? Of course, we must!

We must walk out our sanctification, being infused with His very character. Unconditional love does not mean the Lord approves of everything we do. But He loves us unconditionally above all we may do or not do as we go about our lives.

So why am I being so repetitive? Because it makes all the difference in how we live.

We must "do" out of the firm foundation of His unconditional love, not to earn His favor, but to celebrate it! It is so sad to see our Latter Day Saint neighbors as well as so much of the churches at large either working so hard or just giving up on earning heaven.

Good deeds often are often driven by strings attached as if our good works blackmail God into saving and sanctifying us. The good is done with an emphasis of accumulating heavenly blessings, or to recruit new believers. Even so, I give them full credit for their diligence, but just pray that they can see the simple gospel of salvation by grace through faith. Salvation is simply a gift whereby we move from the house of wrath, the natural consequence of being without God, into the house of love, the natural consequence of being in Him, and He in us.

Jesus is promising them His Holy Spirit's infinite joy. But just as He must walk through the pain of the cross, so will they walk through grief and pain at His loss.

It will be like a birthing room. Trials of life are like a birthing room.

The midwife is God's Holy Spirit, the seed that was planted and is nourished and protected in our spiritual womb, is the Word of God.

This pregnancy will ultimately result in the birthing of a new you and me at some kingdom level. Sons and daughters will be transformed into His likeness with His own image reflecting from our faces just as Christ reflected the exact image of His Father.[116]

The disciples will forget their grief because He is risen. He is risen indeed! He rises again and again in our lives from one level of intimacy to the next as we come to know him ever more intimately. The only way to ride on His wings above the mountains is to be willing to go through the valleys as well.

New levels of empowerment are always forged in the fires of adversity.

Passing through the dark times, we do not long for those shadows again, the lies of the dark deceiver of our souls. Instead, we hear the voice of the Spirit inviting us to, "Stay in the light."

"No one," promises Jesus, "truly no one will be able to take this joy from you. Joy has a name. His name is Jesus, author and finisher of our faith, King of the hidden kingdom which is composed of righteousness, peace and joy. He is the "Bright and Morning Star," the Author of Life springing forth from Eternal Light. He dances over us with joy says Zephaniah, twirling around and around, singing over us! His love Paul exclaims is so wide and long and high and deep that we will never be able to understand or own it.

But His love, once tasted, owns us as we must respond as best we can by surrendering every moment of everyday. He deserves no less, but demands nothing! Amazingly, He is greatly moved by our love so that "one look from our eyes ravishes His heart."[117]

His joy flows from His protective heart covering His bride. He is jealous for us in the highest understanding of the word.

His jealousy is not petty and insecure, rather He loves His bride so much that He would protect her from any usurper who would supplant Him .They can only lie and deceive and ultimately destroy with the seductive adulteress spirit of this age that leaves us raped and ravaged and disillusioned.

Joy cannot be taken, but it can be given away to deceptive enticing lies. The end result is separation from the Lover of our Soul.

What begins as an enticing fragrance soon becomes the familiar stench of death, the decaying and corruption and must be brought to the cross. "As we are faithful to confess or sins before Him, He is faithful and just to forgive."[118] Like Lazarus we walk out as a new man. It is not as hard as we make it, this confession thing. Simply and honestly say, "Forgive me Father, for I have sinned. "

Resurrection Life raises us up once again to walk in Christ's new beginnings.

His joy is connected with Light. Jesus is the light. God spoke, "let there be light," and it was so. Sickness, pain, suffering seem always to be worse at night. "Weeping tarries for the night by joy comes in the morning."

The morning sun coming up signals new possibilities, new beginnings; joy seems synonymous with light. In heaven there is no need for any other sources of light other than the Father and Son, Light with no shadows, joy with no sorrow. No more pain, no more tears.

He was heralded as the Light of the World.

The people who had been in great darkness have now seen a great light, Isaiah said. The angels had "good news with great joy" delivered with the convergence of light that was the Bethlehem Star. This King's kingdom consists of righteousness, peace and joy in the Holy Spirit, triune characteristics emanating from the Triune Godhead, the Three in One, whose light brings "Good News of great joy!" "Joy," as Keven Deadmond has said, "is one third of the kingdom."

The way we remain in His joy, is to remain in Jesus, the Light, even when surrounded by darkness. And though Friday is here in your Passion Week as it were, He will rise with you out of your time of grief.

Joy will break forth like the light of dawn on resurrection morning and manifest new life.

That which you thought dead, is transformed into something so much more than you had even imagined. The King is here for you, and everything is new.

How His church could use an infusion of joy right now! Sadly when joy has come, the critics rose up and said this is over the top.

But that's just it, joy is over the top! It bursts forth in spontaneity; it is not proper and calculated, muted or stifled. Joy bubbles forth. It dances with joy over Jesus, even as Jesus dances with joy over us.

People actually laugh uncontrollably in church, oh my goodness!

There is of course a joy that weeps, but everyone still knows it is joy!

Scripture declares that the joy of the Lord is our strength. Find Jesus, embrace His light and you find joy. Find joy and it is what will fortify and strengthen you even as you walk through dark times.

The cross was the joy set before Him so that we could escape its punishment.

His joy supersedes circumstances.

It is joy like a river, ever flowing and available, joy of the unspeakable kind, and full of grace!

Chapter IX

Ask in His Name

"In that day you will no longer ask Me anything. ***I tell*** ***you the truth,*** *my Father will give you whatever you ask in My name. Until now you have not asked for anything in my name. Ask and you will receive and your joy will be complete,"(John 16:23).*

Previously we have discussed how Jesus wants to complete our joy.

Now we see yet another way that joy will be sustained. Because of His resurrection and subsequent presence among His followers, because He is going back to the Father and will be interceding for His followers, because He will send His Holy Spirit, the Counselor, Comforter and Spirit of Truth and now because He will give us what we ask in His name…our joy will be complete.

Jesus has already promised that, whoever has faith in Him will "do what he has been doing."

We will do even greater things than these because He is going to the Father.

"And I will do whatever you ask in My name, so that the Son may bring glory to the Father, you will ask for anything in My name and I will do it."[119]

Jesus clarifies His promise by saying that He will not need to ask Father on their behalf, rather, they will have a face to face relationship with a Father Who loves them because they have believed that Jesus came from Him. The Father loves you, the Father loves me. We may believe that Jesus loves and died for us, we may have an intellectual knowledge of this love based on John 3:16 but are we immersed in His love to the point that we learn to define ourselves as His beloved?

Do we believe He will give anything that agrees with His promises and purposes in the earth?

We aim so low in our intercession. We barely ask for our unsaved cousin or neighbor.

The Lord says, "Ask of Me and I will give **the nations**."[120] Scripture records whole cities turning to the Lord.

Think about how much you love your own children. Is there blessing you would withhold if it would help them step into their destiny.

Is there anything you would withhold if you knew that it would bless them and others around them?

Is there anything you would withhold of your presence that would renew and restore, revive and revitalize them and, as a result, impact their communities?

Are there those things you would not do, though good in and of themselves which would hinder their growth as persons who are maturing in kingdom character?

How much more is our Father willing to give us His very best?

When we consider God's kingdom perspectives as much as He reveals them to us, answers to prayers may look entirely different than just meeting our need.

Of course, there are those times when our pain is screaming so loudly it is hard to hear anything else. Even then, the Comforter comforts in His own way, if we will draw near and wait.

How critical in this whole endeavor of prayer and intercession, is the ability to listen.

When Jesus prefaces His remarks with "Truly, truly, I say unto you," He is exhorting us to "listen," "I am telling you the truth."

As we grow in our ability to hear His still small voice or hear Him directing us to a scripture, or see a vision or interpret a dream He is a God longing to reveal Himself to us. He is not silent, nor has He ever been silent. He is the Voice of the "deep calling unto deep" that David talked about. His voice is like the sound of many waters, thundering forth or at times, or quietly rippling over the small stones in the river at other times.

Just as it is in any relationship, it is our privilege to seek Him out as a wise man seeks out the treasures in another who is far wiser.

He is the Word, John tells us in his prologue, the Living Word.[121] He is ever speaking forth and ever creatively accomplishing every aspect of the Father's will and desire. It is in His name, the Word of God, through whom all things were created that we ask.

How often do we say, "In Jesus' name" without understanding or authentic faith, but as a rote ending to our requests?

When we end our "prayer in Jesus name," do we realize the responsibility of the power of the One on whose behalf we are speaking?

Ending a prayer in Jesus' name implies we are speaking in His behalf, as His ambassador, His representative, as one who is well acquainted with His purposes and agenda. In Jesus' name is not a handy rote ending to a personal request.

When Jesus speaks the words recorded in John 16:23, He is imparting critical revelation regarding kingdom business.

"Appeal to the Father on the basis of living in My name, having your life centered in all that My name represents, and Father will give you your desire."

Jesus is making an astounding promise here. He is giving power of attorney to His followers, in His name, to transact kingdom business as His ambassadors on earth. This promise is not *carte blanche,* but it is much more than the church has made it to be in our era. If we ask heaven to invade earth the way He taught us to, "Your kingdom come,

Your will be done on earth as it is in heaven," will He not bend His ear to hear and respond? And if He does, what does heaven on earth look like?

Will it not look like heavens dimension that He illustrated for us in Palestine? The lame and blind were healed, the devil oppressed freed, Good News spread to those who needed to hear it the most, and the hungry miraculously fed. He said we would see the kingdom.

This means two things. One, He is saying when the kingdom manifests itself; it is visible, "demonstrable." Believers and unbelievers know something of heaven has been poured out. Someone is changed, someone is healed. There are illustrations of this kind of manifestations in every awakening and revival in church history.

There are illustrations in our time where His kingdom is being manifested in just such ways.

Some Illustrations Of Kingdom Power Today

Thousands of poor are fed and miraculous healings, even resurrections of some dead for hours are being manifested in Mozambique through Roland and Heidi Baker's ministry.

The Lord spoke to them and said if they would reach out to the poor, He would pour out His blessings on them. Several thousand churches have been planted, young pastors trained, people saved and healed.

People come from around the world for healing at Bethel Church in Redding, California. Not all are healed, but many are healed in their prayer rooms.

In Happy Valley where I live, at Destiny Christian Fellowship, over 4,000 people received Christ in a year, and there have been many healings on the street accompanying those decisions for Christ. Leaders are training and releasing lay people to go into the city and reach out with the good news in a caring way.

Teri Gant of Father's Heart Ministry feeds the hungry, prays for and provides shelter for hundreds of homeless in Portland Oregon.

Laurie, my wife, and I went with leaders after a Saturday training session and watched them at work. It's like trolling for souls. They just listened to the Spirit about who to talk to along the way as we made our way over to two mass transportation venues. We watched, then we did some ourselves, then Laurie was cut loose at the bus terminal, we went to the rail transit station around the corner.

Laurie led five people in the sinner's prayer, nearly all teens or college age, and we also led about four to confess Christ. Young people are particularly open to the gospel right now. They see the world falling apart around them.

There is a shift in regard to spiritual hunger that the church must step into.

There are other avenues of power available. Sadly, because of this void, having not heard the pure Word of the Gospel, having not seen the power of the gospel, young people are turning to the dark side.

Part of this very simple direct approach, is praying a blessing over people before praying for them to receive Jesus. In that prayer, we listen for words of knowledge or wisdom.

We did not always get specific words, but prayed a general prayer of God's blessings over their lives, His love, His plan for them for good and not evil, that He would prosper them. In short, they feel the love of God being poured out upon them. People need to know that God loves them and wants them to be part of His family.

He sent His son to die for them. When we minister in this manner you could feel people being touched by the Spirit of God, hearts being softened.

 "Pray this prayer after me: Jesus…" and we would lead them in the sinner's prayer. What we are seeing is that as we declare the word that God loves us and has good plans for our lives, but scripture says, "that all have sinned and fallen short of the glory of God,"[122] that it **is,** "the power of God unto salvation"[123] just as Paul the Apostle said.

We ask them the critical question of their eternal destination and most are not able to affirm that they would be with Jesus if I they died right now. The free gift of God is salvation through Christ Jesus.

Believers need to see what a great gift and what good news this is! Many of their eyes are opened to their need for God in ways that merely talking to them about their spiritual status or whether they believe there is a God will not do.

Much prayer is needed for this kind of outpouring. Much seed has already been sowed, and it is time for harvest!

May the Lord of Harvest send forth His reapers. May the Lord pour out His Spirit of boldness upon each one of His believers.

May these outpourings spread like wildfire!

Spiritual Eyes

The second thing Jesus is saying when He says we will "see" His kingdom, is that He is giving us spiritual eyes, ways of seeing into the spirit realm through the empowerment of His Spirit. In other words, He is speaking to us in word pictures like photographic pictures that are prophetic in meaning, that they edify, encourage and exhort the body of Christ and, (this is a big **and)** they bring revelation while we touch unsaved souls on the street!

The gifts of the Spirit were given not only to edify the church, but to impart to us "power from on high" Jesus said.[124]

The Holy Spirit will show the interns at Bethel in Redding what place to go and minister on Friday nights. Sometimes He will even show them in a vision who it is they will meet.

He will give revelation to the group in "Treasure Hunts" as one approach is called, wherein direction is given collectively regarding where to go and who will be touched by prayer.

My wife and I were on a treasure hunt. As a group we prayed, and several visual pictures were received. We knew to look for a woman in Penny's, in the jewelry department, with red hair, a red baseball cap, and red sweatshirt. As we entered the store at the Town Center, there she was in the jewelry department. She was a nominal believer and rather cold to us at first. Then she opened up and shared that her son was in Afghanistan and she wanted prayer for him.

Then, we found out that one of our group standing apart from the two ministering, had not told us that he got a name as we were praying beforehand. Yeah, you guessed it, it was her name. When my wife showed her the paper with her name on it she was open to more prayer for her own spiritual life.

Another approach was taught to us by Jeanine Rodregas, where we would go as a group to a public area, and as the Spirit led us we would just look for people to encourage without using scripture or Christian Language.

We of course were asking the Spirit for words of knowledge or words of wisdom, both spiritual gifts available to believers now (if you read 1 Corinthians 12 without preconceptions). If you are unfamiliar with these gifts, "words of knowledge" have to do with receiving revelation about things you would not otherwise know in the natural.

Words of wisdom have more to do with how to use that knowledge.

The idea is, of course, that as we encouraged people, it would open up opportunities to share about the Lord. Reports afterward showed that the Holy Spirit was leading us to people and leading our words of encouragement as well. Some people were blessed by two of our groups at the mall. Jeanine established a relationship with a gal at a hair salon whereby they were going to start e-mailing and of course, that would open up thè opportunity for Jeanine to share her experiences with the Lord.

Jeanine simply encouraged her that there was a great future for her and that a pathway was going to be revealed whereby she could use her musical talent (the knowledge of which came to Jeanine without the girl having revealed it, as Jeanine was talking to her).

But what if I pray and I do not see the answer to my prayer and new unforeseen difficulties come?

What if I pray and I seemingly receive no direction about what to do or where to go?

What if?

Often we already have our marching orders. We pray the word over our situations and if he answers a specific need blessed be His Name.

If He apparently does not and says no, or perhaps wait, "blessed be His Name."

"Though He slay me," Job said, "still I will trust Him."

We cannot always explain why a healing does not come when we want one. We, however, can be contenders. But we can stand on the word and "having done all, to stand, and continue to stand,"[125] as Paul said.

We can chose to live in the light of His presence where the fullness of unconditional love resides, resting assured that whatever He does or does not do, He loves us with an unfathomable love. He is working all things out for our good. **He** is the answer, the foundational answer to every prayer.

Even no means yes for our future and destiny. While saying no to one thing He is saying yes to something better from the kingdom perspective. Why? Scripture says in Jesus, "all our promises find their yes."[126]

Something better waits. Even in the valley of the shadow of death for us or a loved one, something better awaits. When overwhelmed with sorrow or grief, something better awaits and His Comforter comforts us in ways only He can.

Completed joy and peace await the one who abandons himself or herself to Jesus because Joy is here, and Peace, and His name is Jesus. He will be our guide in sorrow so we do not lose our peace and our joy in this world in which we will have trouble. But take heart, because He has overcome the world.

He will guide us in the adventure that following Him really is. Ravi Zacharias said, "the believer lives in perpetual novelty."

Forget all the hedging that we have traditionally done around this promise, you know, "Well He can't really mean He'll do whatever you ask." Join with those who relish the adventure of praying, getting the mind of God, then going out led by His Spirit to pray for those who the Spirit reveals, those who need healing, salvation or both, perhaps at the local Starbucks.

How about asking that your home become a lighthouse of prayer and healing in your neighborhood so you could see a move of God flowing from your own home? '

Will He not pour out more blessings than we could imagine if we pray to bless others, blessings that are pressed down shaken together and running over as we reach out to the needy?

We must lift our vision higher.

Smith Wigglesworth said, "There is nothing impossible with God. All the impossibility is with us when we measure God by the limitations of our own unbelief."

Ouch!

Paul prays that "the eyes of our hearts would be enlightened in order that we may know the hope to which he has called us and the riches of His glorious inheritance in the saints, and His **incomparably great power in those who believe."**

"Whatever you ask in My name, that will I do. Whatever you ask the Father in My name, He will do it."

The same power that raised Christ from the dead is available now to Christ's church because He is ascended and He is glorified and He is going forth "conquering and to conquer."

> He is seated at His (the Father) right hand in the heavenly realms, far above all rule and authority, and dominion, and every title that can be given, not only in the present age, but also the age to come. And God placed all things under His feet and appointed Him head over everything for the church, which is his body, the fullness of Him who fills all in all.[127]

What will bring us lasting joy and peace?

Believing at last, even though imperfectly, with warts and all, even though we at times may leave Him as the disciples were about to do that He never leaves us!

Authentic peace and joy come from the Prince of Peace and the Father who invites us into his house of love.

He dances over us with joy and imparts joy unspeakable and full of grace. And our joy is complete because of Father's love, and because we can ask Him for anything that pertains to the authority and power of His Son, our Savior, and He will give it to us His children. Where His good news is being declared, He seems to delight in heaven invading earth.

May we align with heaven's plans and purposes so that our joy may be complete.

Chapter X

Do you love Me? Feed my Sheep

"Feed my sheep. Truly I say this to you, when you were young you girded yourself and walked where you would; but when you are old, you will stretch out your hands and another will bind you and carry you where you do not wish to go (This He said to show by what death he was to glorify God). And after this He said to Him, "Follow Me." John 21:18

When God asks a question, it is not because He does not know the answer!

He knew Peter loved him. He wanted Peter to know that He knew that. He wanted Peter himself to understand that even though he failed, He did then and does still love Him.

It was love that would sustain Peter through the years. Christ's love is in fact the only thing that will carry us and sustain us through years of following Jesus, through the valleys and mountains of our journey. His love for us and our response of love towards Him will be the glue that keeps us close to Him. Nothing else compares. It is not for a church, principles or laws that followers will give their lives; it is only their passion for the Lover of our Soul who loves us even in our failures.

This particular post resurrection scene has always been encouraging for me personally because of the redeeming quality of Jesus' conversation with Peter. Peter had gone back to what He knew before Jesus, fishing. But the resurrected Christ was not about to let him give up on the destiny into which Jesus had prophetically spoken.

"You shall be fishers of men. You are Peter the Rock, and on this Rock I will build my church."

The later words of declaration were spoken after Peter's "spot on" answer to Jesus question, "who do you say I am?"

In the synoptic gospels Peter's great confession comes before Jesus is seen in His brilliant glory in what is called His transfiguration. In that experience with James and John, after Peter's fumbling suggestion of setting up three tabernacles; one for Jesus, Moses and Elijah, God speaks audibly saying, "This is my beloved Son, listen to Him."[128]

What an indelible stamp of Jesus' divine approval Peter experienced as He saw Jesus glorified.

But, somehow, it was not enough to cause Him to stand for Jesus when his own life was on the line. So tragically he had denied Jesus, yet, in this last scene before Jesus' ascension, Jesus wants to catch up with Peter, to close up Peter's gaping wound of guilt and to renew his calling towards his destiny.

Jesus would not deny him or release him from his destiny. He would not allow him to simply go back to what was safe, what he knew best, his default, pre-Jesus place.

This interaction, of course, was not lost on the other disciples who also had left him after Gethsemane. But Peter had of been the most vocal in his claim to lay down his life for Jesus.

Not knowing the full extent of what that meant, he would have every opportunity to live the rest of his life for Christ even after failing in his first challenge.

Here Jesus does affirm that Peter would, in fact, lay down his life even as He declared, being bound and "led where he did not choose to go."

That is what happens when you are following someone whose discipleship training includes certainty of death, one way or the other.

We finds ourselves laying down our own agenda and adopting Jesus' agenda, dying out to our own kingdom as it were, and choosing to be willing subjects in His kingdom.

For many in church history, more and more in our day, this process has necessitated actual martyrdom. And so it did for every single apostle accept John who died a natural death (Some legends claim that they tried to kill him many times, he just would not die).

From history it is know that the Apostle Peter was martyred in Rome around the same time as Paul. Peter faced crucifixion rather than beheading, the method for Paul, a Roman citizen. However, he thought himself unworthy to be crucified like Jesus and chose to be hung on a cross upside down.

But both lived lives totally dedicated to Christ and His kingdom. Both had a pre-Jesus "past," stories of their failures. Jesus seems to like people with stories, and failures.

He sees learners, not failures. He is attracted to those who know how much they have need of a Savior.

Peter, known as Simon, actually started out with a measure of humility.

After experiencing a miraculous catch of fish when Jesus first meets him and the other disciples, he exclaims, "Go away from me Jesus, for I am a sinful man." Between that encounter and this last recorded encounter, something had changed in Simon.

He knew he had failed spectacularly. But now, He does not want Jesus to go away. He, like all the others was shattered when they experienced the apparent end of Jesus' life and ministry. And even though he has gone back to what he knew, pre-Jesus, something has happened at a core level that has redefined him.

He has found out that this Son of God is also Son of Man, and as Son of Man, He empathizes and sympathizes with our frailties. Instead of judging us unworthy of fellowship with the perfect Son of God by reason of our failures, he reaches out as Son of Man, totally identifies with our human experiences, and demonstrates in these same "earth suits" the only model we have of what we are to look like as fully restored human beings. By His life and ministry, the One who could rightfully judge our failures as just reasons for wrath and punishment, or at least penance, instead invites us to come to Him for grace and mercy.

After having gone back to fishing, Jesus suddenly appears on shore asking a familiar question. Children, have you caught any fish?

As soon as John said it was Jesus calling out to them, Peter jumped in the water leaving the other disciples to deal with the super abundance of fish. He could not wait to see Jesus! You would think his guilt would have made him hesitant. The account states that this is the third time Jesus had appeared to them. Peter knows he will find grace and mercy at the very least. But like the Prodigal Father, Jesus has no time for confessions.

He already knew Peter's heart. He wants Peter to see that He does know Peter loves Him even though he failed.

Moreover, **Jesus was not letting any of them off the hook regarding the destiny He had spoken into their lives.**

They all had been told they would be fishers of men. To accentuate that promise in their first meeting, He gives them enough fish miraculously to nearly sink two boats.

Here, His abundant blessing prohibits them from even hauling in the net. They had to tow it in. When Peter got to shore, Jesus asked for more fish to cook them breakfast, Peter goes back to help and counts one hundred fifty fish, yet the net was not torn, another miracle.

At this point no one dared ask, "Who are you?" He had made it plain Who He was.

I believe it was a very abundant blessing meant to remind them of the first time they had met. I believe with that memory comes the reminder of their calling and destiny to fish for souls...and with it the promise of a miraculous abundance of souls for which only God could be praised, not their own skills and abilities.

In short, they are not disqualified from their mission due to their failure to be there for Jesus when he needed them. **He is affirming that he will always be there for them blessing them in abundance even with their failures!**

Because Peter is the point man, Jesus makes it abundantly clear that he is still Jesus' man.

Never did he deny that Peter loved Him in this discourse. Make what you will of the different Greek words, Jesus uses *agape*, Peter, *phileo* usually friendship kind of love. Many scholars say in John's Gospel they are used interchangeably. Still, knowing all things, Jesus knows Peter's love is peppered with holes, just like yours and mine, but He still is Jesus' man. Remember when He told Peter about his immanent denial, He promised He would be praying for Peter. That is why I love this story. Jesus is not about to let our failures block our calling. If we walk away from our destiny, we are going to have to willfully turn away in disobedience and stay there because Jesus' whole method of operation is restoration and renewal. One poet calls Him "the Hound of Heaven."

Why is He so persistent?

Does He only have one "go to" guy?

Can He choose someone else?

The answer is no, He chose you. The word says "the call and anointing of God is irrevocable." Others are chosen for other purposes. The first and highest reason for His persistence is that He loves us so completely and sees us already formed into the person He has destined us to be. He will do everything necessary to get us into that glorious place of destiny.

Secondly, the words He speaks are to us, to propel us forward like the tip of the sword in His hand so that we will by His skill, power, and our cooperation, hit the mark, the high calling to which Jesus has called us.

If we are so yielded to His right arm, we will be shot forth like an arrow to fulfill the calling for which we were created and redeemed.

So Peter was to be the point man of the church's development, the foundation of which is Christ the Messiah, the Son of the living God. From that foundation rises up the truth that Peter expounds in his letters to the churches that we are all living stones, Christ being the Chief Corner Stone, the foundation from which all truths spring forth.

If we are all living stones of this edifice called the church, then Christ's life is pulsating through each living stone, or each body part, each of us having been given our own gifts to match our destiny. All of the combined gifts and destiny's flow together so that the building and body reflect the very person and beauty of Christ. This way, the church will be properly built up and constructed in His likeness so we attract others to Him with the worship of lives lived in joyful obedience, albeit, not always perfect obedience.

We must not give up on each other or ourselves when we fail. Jesus never gives up on us.

Peter's mission for this baby church is to "feed" the sheep of the Head Shepherd. Jesus still believes in him, even if he does not believe in himself. He is gone fishing after all.

Back to what he knew before he encountered Jesus. But when Jesus shows up Peter is smart enough to go to the only place mercy is found. As I mentioned in a previous chapter, Judas did not seem to understand that Jesus is longsuffering and well able to forgive.

Sadly, he hung himself in despair! Here is part of the truth that Peter would need to feed the sheep. Jesus has conquered and is conquering still so that "as He is in the world, so are we." [129]

He has overcome, so we are more than conquerors! He has given us tools that are "mighty for the tearing down of strongholds."[130]

It is these mindsets, many of which are from the lies of the enemy of our souls, fiery darts which are meant to derail us from our destiny in Christ. What will we confess over ourselves? One of the most insidious lies of the enemy is a false humility that basically says we are junk, unworthy of assignment in the Army of the King.

Jesus said to Peter at his great confession that the gates of hell would not be able to prevail against the church. In Peter's case the enemy would want to cause him to declare over himself that he is a failure. But the truth is, he is the Rock, who failed having been afraid. He learned humility through that experience and he still is the leader upon which Jesus is about to build His church.

Remember, it was Peter, whom Jesus said the devil desired to sift, who encourages us later in his letter to the churches that we should not think it strange that we run into opposition, persecution, or attack for the sake of the gospel. We are to keep our eyes fixed on Jesus with whom we will become partners in His suffering, so we also will be partners in His glory. So we are to be happy when insulted for being a follower of Christ because the glorious Spirit of God will come upon us.[131] We are to take a firm stand against the enemy, the devil who prowls around like a lion looking for victims.

One of the ways we take our stand is to believe and declare the Word of God and Who He says we are, rather than agreeing with circumstances or with the deceiver and liar.

That does not mean we deny our circumstances, it means we recognize a higher truth that is working in our behalf.

It is that higher truth we must lay hold of. What we believe now empowers God's Spirit to create future experiences in our adventure of following Jesus.

Faith comes by hearing the "Faith-giver" speak into our lives. As we speak forth His words, He moves in the invisible realm to activate those promises. Hope keeps those promises ever before us until we see the Spirit of Christ fulfill them. Jesus was telling Peter that he would see the church birthed shortly. Then he was to feed these three thousand souls ushered in by the Spirit's outpouring at Pentecost. Peter would still be the voice Jesus would use.

Abraham believed God's promise when it was not logical to do so and "called things that were not as though they were,"[132] Paul teaches us. Remember who it is that we are following.

"In the beginning was the Word, the Word was with God" and this same Word created all things. He still "creates" on behalf of those who will allow Him to be the "High Priest of their confession"[133] as the Hebrew writer calls Him. The question is, are we giving Him anything to work with? Like tithing, we must give him something to multiply.

Are we cooperating with Him by declaring His promises which have been ignited in our spirit by His Spirit, over our lives?

How many of us have also hung up our calling and destiny by disqualifying ourselves by reason of failure when the Lord has not done so? Maybe we have not disqualified ourselves, perhaps we have felt disqualified by others, rejected. Perhaps things did not turn out the way we thought they should.

That was surely true for the disciples. Perhaps disillusionment and disappointment have even turned to bitterness. Maybe we were hurt deeply, even betrayed and now we are afraid we'll get hurt again. Jesus was hurt, and betrayed before us. He knows what we are going through.

"He came unto His own and His own received Him not." "He was rejected and despised, a man of sorrows, acquainted with grief."[134]

Perhaps you think your age is an inhibiting factor, you're too old or too young.

In this new era of healthier pre-retirees and retirees we need to ask the Lord how He can still use us. What sheep are we to feed, saved or unsaved, that Jesus wants us to bless as we have been blessed. His mercies are new every morning.

I was reading last night in the Parade magazine about several teens who have started non-profit agencies that help the poor here and in other countries. What creative and effective ideas! I need some of that entrepreneurial spirit.

Jesus summed up by challenging Peter to follow Him, after declaring in what manner Peter would be martyred. Jesus never hides the truth. He told His disciples He would die for the sins of all mankind and they did not hear it. It was too unbelievable for them.

Here He invites Peter to follow Him by telling him how he will also die for the sake of the gospel. What a job description!

Feed my sheep which is no easy task, and die for doing it! Peter must have been feeling somewhat overwhelmed because he redirects Jesus to John asking, "What about him?" Jesus responds by saying, my plan for John is of no concern to you. You just keep following Me Peter.

That is really what it is about, is it not?

Keep on following, even when we slip and fall, fail miserably, or miss the mark terribly.

Psalm 84 refers to a heart pilgrimage on the highway to the dwelling place of the Lord, in which we will go through the Valley of Baca (which means weeping), but it will be turned into a place of springs, of fruitfulness.[135]

In this process David says we will go from strength to strength. Sometimes we don't feel that is what is happening. But remember, Paul said it was in His weakness that Jesus made him strong. Because we slip and fall does not mean we are off the pathway.

A righteous man slips and falls and gets up seven times.[136]

The question is, will we keep following and keep fighting the good fight.

Will we contend for the truth?

David goes on to say "better is one day in the courts of the Lord than thousands elsewhere."[137] That is the truth!

Conclusion

One of the predominate truths Jesus offers to us in these statements in John's Gospel is that He calls us to Himself, not to a religion.

We enter into relationship with Him through a radical birth into a new existence called His kingdom. We have a new spiritual DNA, a new heredity, a new destiny if we can receive it.

He did not merely deal with sins; He dealt a deathblow to "Sin" in us. We are now "the righteousness of God" in Christ Jesus.

Paul later says in Colossians for us to "put on" our new nature, that new person which is being renewed daily in the knowledge and image of Christ.[138] To put it on does not equate to hypocrisy, rather, we embrace our new nature and walk it out in our daily lives empowered by His Spirit. His laws are now in our new heart, given to us by receiving Him. **He has made us into much more than we have ever imagined.**

We were sinners. We have been saved by grace. We are now saints of God. Because we love Him, we pursue and protect our Father's heart. In fact, we are now a part of the Trinitarian love triangle, the Three in One fellowship, His Spirit abiding in each of us.

He has given us new eyes with which to see and new ears with which we hear His voice of guidance. In this New Kingdom, listening is of the highest priority. "Listen to me, says the Lord, I am telling you the truth."

How blessed for us to have both His written word and His continually speaking Word.

Faith comes by hearing the "Faith-Giver," speak.[139] So often we cannot see what is ahead, but God's Spirit guides us even through the darkness.

He is the Light of Life.

The kingdom of God is knowable and notable.

Knowing is experiential in Hebrew and Christian thought. The promise of God is that signs and wonders will follow the preaching of the good news! He has given us witnessing gifts as resources of His Spirit to share with those we touch daily, at home, in our neighborhoods, and in the marketplace.

Jesus said we would do greater things than He. Now multitudes of believers are filled with His empowering Spirit and are able to be in multiple locations simultaneously living and sharing the Good News! As His disciples, we are nations within nations reflecting His light and His glory in redemptions' transforming story.

We are His ambassadors affecting kingdom strategies of restoration to God's original plan and purposes on earth.

Our mindset "should we choose to accept this mission" is one of genuine humility exhibited by Jesus who said I only do and say what the Father is doing and saying. So when He offended religious sensitivities by healing on the Sabbath, His answer was that His Father is always working for good, so also is He.

He shatters our religious mindsets that would keep Him in a box of predictability, and calls us to look intently into His eyes for healing and deliverance from our imprisoning limitations. He then challenges us to, "get up, and pick up our mats and walk," taking the first steps of faith as the Faith-giver speaks liberation and freedom to us.

We are then privileged to exhibit in humility the trophies of our deliverance that they might become testimonies of His goodness which draw others to Him.

As His ambassadors we must fully embrace His perspective rather than any other false perspective of who we are as His family.

Then just as the paralytic did, we transparently exhibit the testimony of our deliverance in order to bring hope to others.

It is in our weaknesses that Christ's strength is perfected. So we need not live in denial, rather we always point to the One Who is our, acknowledging that we can do all things through Christ who strengthens us.

We must ask ourselves how our own preconceptions are inhibiting Christ from having His way in us. Are we missing His current moving because we are too busy looking back at the past. We must take our eyes off the pool as it were, and look to the, "One who gives life to whom He is pleased to give"

Jesus declares that He is the only way that we will ever find real peace and satisfaction.

While some followed because He miraculously fed them, He called them to a higher level so that they could see that He is the Bread that has come down from heaven by which their eternal and finite needs will be met. He did this in such a shockingly emphatic way that many of His disciples turned away and stopped following Him having misunderstood His teaching. The statements Jesus made are even today a magnificent call to intimacy.

He is calling us to hunger and thirst after Him, to drink from Him, the fountain of life, to partake of Him.

He is the True Bread from heaven. Unless we feast on Him we will be spiritually malnourished. We will eat but not be filled. We will drink but our thirst will not be slated.

Only He can supply that for which we essentially ache, relationship with the One who created us and longs to be with us.

Christ Jesus as the Bread of Heaven infuses us with eternal life which begins now, in our present time, and with eternal destiny.

We are sent to be bread to the nations and in our circle of influence even as Christ was.

As He received his words from the Father, so we receive from the Living Word sharing this bread with the nations. As He was broken and poured out, so we are broken and poured out as living sacrifices, our "reasonable worship" as Paul later calls this process.[140]

But if we have not been partaking of Him, rather than bread from heaven, we can only give that which is dry and stale reflecting the condition of our heart.

Jesus uses another powerful metaphor as He reveals Himself to those who seek Him, even those looking to entrap Him. He is the "Light of the World." He is the brilliant light that Isaiah foretold prophesying that, "the people in darkness have seen a Great Light."

He promises that those who walk in His light will experience the Light of Life.

This discourse unfolds as a skillfully written contrast between the brilliant light of relationship with Christ, contrasted with the darkness of religion, mans efforts to make himself right with God.

Religion results in several destructive and unsatisfying outcomes. One, they were living on previous revelation while fresh revelation stood before them in the person of Christ.

Fresh Manna must be gathered daily, or to stay within this metaphor of light, we need light therapy daily to dispel darkness.

Two, those reliant on religiosity rather than relationship appeal to right standing by reason, to being affiliated with the right temple, or the right heritage (sons of Abraham). Relationship with Jesus only provides our righteousness.

Three, a spirit of religiosity is very hard to expose because those afflicted by it think they are the only ones who are right.

Relationship pursues genuine humility and a teachable spirit.

Four, those bound by this spirit do not realize they are in bondage or they are in denial because their bondage has become a safe and comfortable place.

They, in fact, call bondage freedom, they are so deceived. Only the truth of Jesus will "set us free."

Five, religion would rather believe a lie than risk relationship. Countless believers would testify it is worth the risk.

Six, those caught up in religiosity unknowingly serve their father, the liar of liars, who has nothing to do with truth. He is a murderer.

Those who follow him will murder the truth at some level. The more illumination and revelation Jesus brought, the more they desired to kill Him.

Seven, religiosity will go so far as assigning what is of God to the devil.

Jesus invites us to stay in the light of His continuing revelation. In the very next scene, a man who was blind from birth is healed by Jesus and immediately testifies before religious leaders that it is obvious that this Healer is from God.

"As long as I am in the world, I am the Light of the world."

Hear Jesus calling us to more and more revelation and illumination as He shines on us, in us and through us even in the darkest moments of our lives. Even darkness is as light to Him.[141]

The claims of Jesus regarding Himself are astounding. No other teacher in history has said "Come to Me, I am the Way, I am the Truth, I am the Life." His invitation is all inclusive, but his direction regarding how to find truth is exclusive.

There is only one avenue to God the Father, who declares Himself the One and only God multiple times in the law and the prophets. That way is through the "door" of His Son whom He sent for the salvation of all mankind. He is the entry way, and He is the "Good Shepherd of His Kingdom flock.

His sheep follow only Him. They know His Voice only. He lays down His life for them, feeding, protecting, and keeping them free from parasites and disease by leading them to pure water. Other "doors" and "shepherds" exact burdensome ritual and appeasement through which one is never sure if they are pleasing and acceptable or not.

It is His goodness that caused thousands to believe and receive Him as Savior and Lord as He ministered in Palestine.

It is evermore His goodness that transforms people's lives as they experience unconditional love from the One who made it possible. It is His kindness that leads to repentance. In this love we experience His promise of continued revelation, we hear His voice.

He gives us eternal life as we believe in Him. As a result we will never perish.

No one will be able to snatch us out of His hand!

He can make these promises only because as He declares, "I and the Father are One." He is co-equal with God. Therefore, He is by divine right the only Way, Truth and Life.

He is jealous for us as any good husband would be. He guards His beloved from any deceiving encroaching shepherd. His love never fails and never gives up on His beloved. He gently leads those who are with young.

With His unfailing love He conquerors our hearts.

But He conquers in a most paradoxical way: By giving His life for us taking our sin and shame, our pain and sorrow, our infirmities and volunteering to stand in for us as a substitute, paying the just requirement for sin—death. He declares that unless a grain of wheat goes into the ground, it remains only one grain. But by dying in the ground, it springs forth into a life giving plant.

First comes the stalk, then the blade, then the grain to be harvested and turned into bread for sustaining life. It is through dying that He can produce many seeds which in turn can become bread for the nations.

This was His mission as "Son of Man."

This was how He displayed power, the antithesis of earth's power brokers.

When some Greeks sent word that they wanted to "see Jesus," He responded by saying, as it were, "let them see me in the context of my mission as Son of Man."

By losing His life, eternal life is gained for all who will lose their lives also by submitting to Him even as He was submitted to His Father.

See Him as the first fruit of abundant fruitfulness through those who believe and obey. See Him as having rendered judgment upon this world and the worlds system of fear and intimidation sponsored by the fear monger, Satan who, though still among us, is ultimately defeated. See Christ as "lifted up" having become a curse so we could live free from the curse of the law and the cross.

He challenges them and us, to walk in the light of this revelation. The way up was down for the Son of Man.

So it is for His own who would die to their old nature and put on the new, rising up from death as grain, bread which is broken for the nations.

To further illustrate Jesus' authentic humility, He calls together his closest disciples at a last meal in Jerusalem and humbles Himself in a shocking way to illustrate how His believers should function in His kingdom.

He grabs a towel and a bowel and washes their feet. He did this to, "show them the full extent of His love for them."

Peter objects strongly to Jesus performing this lowly act for him. But Jesus says let me, or you will have no part of me.

Peter responds that Jesus could wash all of Him but Jesus says no, He is clean except for His feet. How we each need his daily washing away the grime of this world as we walk among its corruption.

So what will we do with a God who washes our feet?

Peter accepts Jesus' cleansing. Hopefully He remembers this as he is told to listen to the truth, that he will betray Jesus several times.

Judas having also been washed seems not to have recalled what Jesus here illustrates, how he offers cleansing, how mercy triumphs over judgment. Peter receives Christ's pardon and encouragement to, "feed His sheep." But Judas destroys himself in grief. Peter steps into His destiny as one of the early church pillars. Judas remains the quintessential symbol of betrayal.

Jesus said listen to the truth that no servant is greater than His master. He placed Himself under complete subservience to His Father as Master in His earthly mission.

So must we.

So we are able joyfully to do so as we see more and more of His goodness. But He warned that as He was persecuted, so will we also be. But He will send His indwelling Spirit to encourage and inspire boldness to fearlessly proclaim the "Good News."

Let us hear Him speak our name of destiny to us even as He did to Peter, the "Rock," and let us step into that destiny having been called out by the One who washes our feet.

Jesus had been honest with his disciples all along and shared that they will experience great grief very soon and while others rejoice, they will weep. In this brief statement He compares what they will go through as participants of His death to a mother bravely experiencing childbirth.

They will be in great pain, but when the child comes forth, the pain will be forgotten having been completely superseded by the joy of new life. They will ultimately see their Messiah again after resurrection.

So it is with all saints who go through times of loss and grief. If we allow the Holy Spirit to be our guide, we will come out of the process changed and transformed into new levels of life in Christ. Scripture declares that there are hidden treasures to be found in the dark places of our lives.[142]

In our pain we focus only on relief. In the midst of grief we wonder if life will ever be the same. When we have lost our way, our vision, or our dreams have fallen apart we wonder where the Lord is. If we will sit and break bread with Him as the Emmaus travelers did, perhaps we also will finally be aware of His ever continuing presence. He has been with us all along.

"Surely this is none other than the house of the Lord" Jacob said at Bethel, "and we did not know it."

As the Afro-American pastor preached, "Friday is here, but Sunday is coming!"

Resurrection life is bursting forth like the lily of the valley. Our grief will turn to joy in time.

He will turn our mourning into dancing.

We will wonder at His appearing in our lives as if He suddenly materialized in our hearts as He did in the room where His disciples hid in fear and disillusionment. He will bring astounding new hope of new possibilities. He will not release us from our destiny!

In order to fulfill that destiny, Jesus offers another astounding promise couched within the context of completing our joy. "I tell you the truth, my Father will give you whatever you ask in my name…ask and you will receive and your joy will be complete." He is giving us authority to transact kingdom business in His name, as His ambassadors on earth.

We can appeal to the Father based on living in "His name," having our lives centered in all that His name represents, all that His will in the earth would heal and restore, and He will give us our desire!

All this is understood in the context of unconditional love. As a parent what gift would you withhold that would simply bring joy to your child? What gift, on the other hand, would you withhold, if it would somehow jeopardize their character, and thus, their ability to enter into the fullness of their destiny? When we consider God's kingdom purposes, answers to prayer may look different than expected. But God is good all the time. Jesus elsewhere says He does not give counterfeits.

Our key attitude must be one of listening for the voice that at times "shatters the cedars of Lebanon," and at other times is, "the still small voice" that spoke to Elijah. Praying in His name means, "His will be done on earth as in heaven." We are not bereft of revelation. Often our prayers are week relying on, "if it be your will," as if we cannot know His will. More often than not His will is available if we but seek. We spend too much time praying for what we already have "in Christ."

What draws His heart more than anything else is to hear cries for His presence to come and impact our whole communities and cities.

How we need another "Great Awakening" in America! Our remedy is not political as we near yet another presidential election this fall. That does not mean we should not exercise our responsibility to vote as many Christians sadly do. We need God to sweep over this nation city by city as He has done before.

Do it again Lord!

But it is not someone else who will do it. He works through his entire family, his church individually and corporately.

We must awaken to our authority in Christ!

When His kingdom comes, it is both knowable and notable. He will confirm the "Good News" with signs and wonders as He promised.

"Those who know their God will do great exploits." Paul says for those who will believe, there is available an "incomparably great power," from the same source that raised Jesus from the dead! We see it today in many third world countries. Why not here in America? Nothing else can bring that kind of lasting joy, to see heaven invade earth!

Let it be so, O Lord!

What happens when we fail? Does Jesus turn His back on us?

No He does not give up on His family.

When Peter failed so spectacularly, denying Jesus, Jesus appeared to him after resurrection and reaffirmed His call and destiny. Even before Peter's denial of Jesus, the Lord promised that He would pray for Peter. How encouraging and directly related to how Peter handled his failure. He ran to Jesus, not away from Him in despair like Judas did. Peter seemed to know something about Jesus that Judas had not learned even though Jesus loved him until his suicide.

Peter had gone back to fishing. But Jesus did not disqualify him from his destiny as the point man of the early church. In Jesus' perspective, Peter is still the Rock.

How encouraging. We must stop listening to our "soulish" thoughts of guilt and shame after having come to Jesus where we find grace and mercy in time of need.

He "separates our sin from Him as far as the east is from the west." "There is therefore, now no condemnation for those who are in Christ Jesus!"

He will not allow our failure to block our calling and destiny if we will not allow it. There are sheep to be fed. But that calling will include persecution of various kinds and death at one level or another.

For Peter it would be martyrdom. For us, dying to our old nature and embracing the new person Jesus has created us to be and become. Perhaps, like Peter, we also will be led where we would not choose to go. But in the end, better is one day in the courts of the Lord than thousands elsewhere!

Our challenge is to follow the One who is true, the One who is truth, and always speaks the truth, the one who will never forsake us or leave us! In His presence is fullness of joy!

"Truly, Truly I say unto you....."

Larry and Laurie Kennedy, their three daughters and five grandchildren reside in the Pacific Northwest.

For the past 35 years, Larry has ministered at several churches as an Associate Pastor, Worship Pastor, song writer, writer, and workshop instructor. He has also lead and taught in Malaysia, Thailand, Mexico, Brazil and Guatemala City.

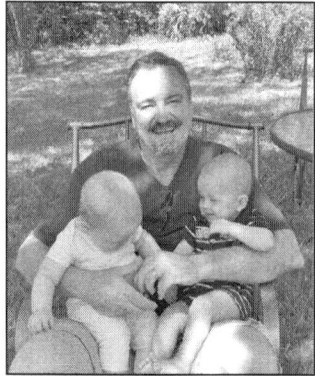

He now ministers in worship at Destiny Christian Fellowship, in Oregon.

Larry excels in dynamic and intimate worship. His love for the Lord and heart for transformative worship shines through as he leads and teaches.

His formal training comes from Abilene Christian University, Pepperdine University and Warner Pacific College where he received his Master's degree in biblical studies in 2004.

His most valuable training, by far, has come while sitting at the feet of Jesus in worship.

End Notes

---

[1] *Michael Eyquem de Montaigne*
[2] Isa. 46:19
[3] Eph. 3:10—11
[4] Matthew 18:3
[5] Matthew 19:14
[6] John 8:32
[7] 2 Cor.4:6
[8] 1 Cor. 15:50
[9] 2 Corinthians 5:21
[10] Col. 3:3; Rom. 6:3
[11] Col. 3:9
[12] Rom. 6:6
[13] 1 John 1
[14] Jeremiah 31:33, Ez. 36:26; Heb. 10:16
[15] Eph. 1:1, 2 Cor.1:1
[16] Isa. 30: 21
[17] Eph. 1:20
[18] Psalm. 34:5
[19] Rom. 2:9-10
[20] 1 Cor. 2:16
[21] John 1:16
[22] Rom 8:19
[23] Jo. 3:13
[24] Is. 60
[25] Mark 16:17-18
[26] Matthew 5:6
[27] Is. 61:1
[28] John 5:20-21
[29] John 5:24-25
[30] Philippians 1:6
[31] Pr.23:7
[32] 1 Cor. 1:1

[33] Prov. 28
[34] Daniel 11:32
[35] Prov. 5:20
[36] Philippians 4:13
[37] John 10:5
[38] John 14:12
[39] John 5:24

[41] John 6:33
[42] John 6:47
[43] John 6:54
[44] John 6:68
[45] John 3:16
[46] John 6:57
[47] Jo.4:13
[48] 1 Cor. 11:27-32
[49] 1Cor. 1:30
[50] Gal. 5:22
[51] Is. 54:13
[52] Hebrews 10:19
[53] Heb. 4:16
[54] Open up the Sky – Deluge
[55] Ps16: 11
[56] John 14:9
[57] ICor.4:6
[58] John 15
[59] John 8:32
[60] John 8:34
[61] John 8:48
[62] John 8:51
[63] John 8:58
[64] John 8:30
[65] John 8:24,28
[66] John 9:5

[67] Is. 61:1-3
[68] Isaiah 42:5-8
[69] Jer. 31
[70] 1 Tim 2:5
[71] Acts 4:12
[72] Ps 23:6
[73] John 10:10
[74] Ps 40:6-7
[75] Matthew 19:14
[76] John 10:30
[77] John 10:33
[78] John 14:11
[79] John 10:37
[80] John 12:21
[81] John 12:24
[82] John 12:28
[83] John 12:28
[84] John 12:32
[85] John 12:26
[86] Gal. 3:16; Rom 4:16
[87] Rom 3:26
[88] Eph. 2:8
[89] Eph. 12:33
[90] Deut. 21:23
[91] Gal. 3:12-14
[92] Is. 53:4
[93] Phil Yancy
[94] Heb. 4:16
[95] Col. 2:14
[96] John 12:46
[97] John 1:11
[98] Ps. 22:3
[99] Rev. 1:5

[101] John 13:1
[102] John 21:17
[103] John 21:17
[104] John 13:3
[105] Matthew 26:34
[106] John 13:16
[107] John 11:16
[108] John 13:20
[109] Matthew 26:21
[110] Rev. 6:1
[111] Romans 6:23
[112] Isaiah 45:3
[113] John 16:33
[114] Ps. 42:7
[115] Psalm 103:12
[116] Heb. 1:1-13
[117] Song of Songs 4:9
[118] 1 John 1:9
[119] John 14:12-13
[120] Psalm 2:8
[121] John 1:1
[122] Romans 3:23
[123] Romans 1:16
[124] Acts 1
[125] Ephesians 6:13
[126] 2Cor:1:19
[127] Eph. 1:18-23
[128] Mark 9:7
[129] 1 John 4:17
[130] 2 Corinthians 10:4
[131] 1 Pet. 12-14
[132] Romans 4:17
[133] Hebrews 3:1

[135] Psalm 107:35
[136] Pr. 24:16
[137] Psalm 84:10
[138] Colossians 3:10
[139] Rom. 10:17
[140] Rom. 12:1-3
[141] Ps. 139:12
[142] Isaiah 45:3

/124

Made in the USA
San Bernardino, CA
02 March 2015